AM I AUTISTIC?

A Guide to Autism & Asperger's Self-Diagnosis for Adults

By

Lydia Andal

~~~

2015 Print Edition Published by
New Idealist Limited
London

CONTENTS

'Is This Guide For You?'

This is a guide to autism for adults who think they *might* be autistic and would like to learn more about autism and the road to self-diagnosis and/or formal diagnosis from the view of an autistic person.

This is also a guide for the family members/partners/work colleagues and friends of adults who they suspect might be autistic or a 'bit' autistic.

Please Note: This guide focuses on autistic adults without learning difficulties.

This Guide Is For You If...

• You think you might be autistic yet are reluctant to request a formal diagnosis or have been unable to get a referral for a formal diagnosis

• You have already been diagnosed as autistic/asperger's and want to learn more about autism from the view of an autistic person

• You think your partner/family member/work colleague may be autistic

Important Notice: This guide has not been written by a medical practitioner. It has been written by an autistic journalist and author who has interviewed leading UK and US autism specialists and autistic advocates in order to provide an informative and balanced view of autism. Anyone seeking medical advice on autism diagnosis should seek advice from a medical practitioner.

'Autism Quick Facts'

• Around 1-1.5% of the world's population is autistic

• Most autistic adults are undiagnosed

• Most autistic adults are of average or above average intelligence

• Most autistic adults talk as normal and have excellent command of language

• Most autistic adults do not have learning disabilities

• Many autistic adults have partners, raise children and work

• There are autistic sports people, business people, lawyers, doctors, actors, artists, screenwriters, authors, pop stars, advocates and academics

• As of 2013 the term 'Asperger Syndrome' is being phased out as an official diagnosis in the US; what was once known as 'Asperger's' is now classed as 'Autism'

• Whilst there are specific 'autistic traits', every autistic person is different

• With the advent of online autism tests and guides such as this, self-diagnosis is now a viable option for many autistic people

Note on References: *In the interests of readability all in text references have been kept to a minimum. The sources for the facts and statistics quoted throughout the chapters can be found in the 'References & Further Reading' section at the end of this guide.*

Preface

AM I AUTISTIC?

A GUIDE TO AUTISM & ASPERGER'S SELF-DIAGNOSIS FOR ADULTS

FIRST EDITION

I have never written a book before.

I have edited a magazine.

It's called *The New Idealist.*

*

The magazine - supported by many international contributors - explored a range of themes including Social Mobility and the rising gap between the rich and the poor, the importance of Emotional Intelligence, the rise in Extreme Weather events and…Autism.

The magazine is now on hiatus, in part so that I would have the time to write this guide and work on the website that supports it.

'The Autism Issue' * of *The New Idealist* was published in August 2014 and came about after I read a news story headlined *'Are we ready for a prenatal screening test for autism?'* **.

After reading the headline (and the story), I suspected 'we' are not.

For *The Autism Issue* I interviewed some of the world's best known autism specialists and asked them about the development of prenatal tests for autism (just to clarify; none of those I spoke to were involved with the development of *prenatal* tests, although some were actively involved in researching blood tests to diagnose autism in young children or adults).

After speaking to them and hearing the way they spoke about autism as a 'disorder involving the brain', an 'impairment' and a 'genetic disorder' (amongst other descriptions), I felt like something was seriously wrong.

I'm autistic and I don't identify with the above descriptions.

I have run businesses, led teams, founded several creative ventures and do not have a 'disorder' (genetic or otherwise). I do have certain 'sensory sensitivities' which I cover in Chapters Six and Seven, yet I know I am more than an 'impairment' and that my autistic sensitivities and extra levels of perception are what enable me to capture the details I put into my work – details that other people often seem to miss.

I also know of autistic people with minimal sensory sensitivity who have good jobs, partners and families of their own, and they do not consider themselves 'impaired' *at all.*

The Rise Of Eugenics: Autism Blood Tests & Genetic Testing

In a rather interesting coincidence, as I am finalising this Preface my writing has been interrupted by the 'all things autism' news feed that I subscribe to carrying the story that California based *'Pediatric Bioscience'* has just announced that they plan to launch a $1,000 *pre-pregnancy* blood test for autism later this year.

Pediatric Bioscience Chief Scientific Advisor Judy Van de Water, Ph.D. is the lead researcher for the *'Maternal Autoantibody (MAR) Test'* marketed by the company which can apparently identify a certain 'form' of autism which accounts for around a quarter of the autism spectrum (according to the website). Van de Water developed the blood test for autism after a study on pregnant mothers she conducted found that mothers with certain antibodies were more likely to give birth to a child later diagnosed as autistic.

In the news article, Jan D'Alvise, President and Chief Executive of *Pediatric Bioscience* gives an indication as to why so many autism 'specialists' are interested in finding the genetic basis of autism when she references the potential financial value of such a test: *'The blood test addresses a potential $1.8 billion market'*.

Pediatric Bioscience advocates the use of the test not for pregnant women, but for women *thinking* of getting pregnant to find out whether they are likely to give birth to an autistic baby so that they then have the option to decide whether to get pregnant with a potentially autistic baby – or not.

The test is marketed on the *Pediatric Bioscience* website as follows:

'Its suggested use is for women prior to becoming pregnant as a family planning tool, or immediately after giving birth to allow early behavioral intervention for the newborn.'

The *Pediatric Bioscience* site suggests women *'who are considering In Vitro Fertilization (IVF) to become pregnant may want to consider taking the test before they proceed with the procedure'*.

As this guide is in the final stages of preparation for publication, the debate around the introduction of this test will have to be continued online.

(Those who would like to know more about the MAR test can visit the accompanying website for this guide at www.amiautistic.com for more information about the background and origins of this test along with updates on the progress and impact of this test if it passes clinical trials ahead of launch later this year).

I do wonder what would have happened if there was a *prenatal* test for autism available at the time I was conceived with an accompanying leaflet carrying a description of autism similar to the one *Pediatric Bioscience* uses to describe autism:

'Autism (AU) and Autism spectrum disorders (ASDs) are a group of neurodevelopmental disorders... While the severity of the symptoms varies widely among affected individuals, in most instances these disorders lead to severe cognitive, communicative and social disabilities, and can be devastating to those children afflicted with autism and to their families.' (Summarised description taken from www.pediatricbioscience.com).

In 1980 (when my mother was pregnant with me), if pregnant mothers were told that their unborn child was carrying 'autism genes' which may lead to a 'devastating affliction' similar to that described above, is there is a chance that I - along with hundreds of thousands of other babies - might not have been born?

I want to say *'my mother wouldn't have aborted me if I tested positive for autism genes'.*

But I just can't be sure.

What does this talk of autism prenatal testing have to do with self-diagnosis?

Challenging The Clinical View Of Autism: The Importance Of Self-Diagnosis

In both the UK and the US, autism is medically defined as a 'mental disorder' and those *clinically diagnosed* as autistic – wherever they sit on the spectrum – will be officially classed as having one.

In my opinion; this is not appropriate.

The misinformation and misconceptions about autism and the autism spectrum spread by clinical 'specialists' and the organisations who back them are now being used in order to justify the development of financially lucrative pre-pregnancy/prenatal tests and 'cures' for autism, and are typical of the negative labels that seem to be attached to autism in general.

The medical system does not recognise the strengths, benefits or positives that can come from being autistic and those who identify as autistic and don't want to be officially labelled as having a 'disorder' have only one option:

Self-Diagnosis.

About This Guide

This guide has been written for those who want to find out if they or their partner/relative/friend/work colleague are autistic without going through the clinical process and potentially being labelled as having a 'disorder'.

After exploring the diagnosis options (which I cover in Chapters Six to Eight), I decided that self-diagnosis was the way forward for me as that way I get to decide what being autistic means to me and I am not subject to the 'clinical' view of autism.

Chapter Three discusses *The Autism Spectrum* and how no two autistic people are the same. For those already clinically diagnosed as autistic who find themselves reading this – I hope this guide will encourage you to question the clinical view of autism and claim your own view of what being autistic means to you – wherever you may sit on the spectrum.

This guide opens with a chapter on the challenges faced by the 'professional autistic' (defined as an autistic person who is in paid employment). Whilst this guide is meant for anyone with an interest in finding out more about autism, I specifically draw attention to autistic people who are *employed* in this chapter because my research has highlighted how those who are able to 'hide' their more obvious autistic traits in order to fit into a non-autistic work environment are the ones who have the most difficulty getting formally diagnosed or recognised as being autistic by wider society.

I have heard stories from autistic people who have tried to declare their autistic status in their workplace or social circle only to be met with disbelief or scorn as they don't 'seem' autistic.

Since I published *The Autism Issue*, I myself have also experienced this and this chapter opens this guide in order to address several fundamental misconceptions about autism from the outset.

Behind The Scenes

Researching and publishing *The Autism Issue* in the summer of 2014 was a huge challenge with behind the scenes 'battles', retractions and attempts to subvert the journalistic process abound.

But still it published.

Researching and preparing this guide for publication has also been extremely demanding, with several people trying their very best to discourage me from publishing it unless I let them influence the editorial direction, as it seems that only their own views of autism are acceptable; new ways of thinking about autism are definitely *not* to be encouraged.

As someone who thinks there is room for a wide range of opinions from all sides of the table on a particular topic, I encouraged and explored a raft of views divergent from my own in *The New Idealist* – and left it up to the readers to decide which view they backed.

I have taken a similar approach with this guide and find the total intolerance of a 'different view' of autism from others educated and experienced enough to know better, odd at best and deeply concerning at worst.

But still, this will publish.

*

For the many people who took the time to provide their thoughts, opinions and experiences of autism to me whilst researching this guide – *Thank you.*

For those who know me personally and have taken the time to read many pages on a topic which might not be of complete interest to you – whilst managing to provide me with some very useful feedback – *Thank you.*

*

For those trying their best to suppress my views:

'I don't have all the answers; I just know to ask the questions'

***

All views expressed in this guide are my own

Thank you for reading

L. Andal

Manchester, 18th January 2015

* A link to The Autism Issue can be found at www.amiautistic.com where it is available for download free of charge

**The Guardian Online, 1st May 2014 'Are we ready for a prenatal screening test for autism?'

*** http://www.utsandiego.com/news/2015/jan/15/autism-pediatric-biosciences-antibodies/

Chapter 1

THE PLIGHT OF THE PROFESSIONAL AUTISTIC

If you are a 'Professional' autistic who has a career and lives independently yet struggles to manage some of your autistic traits; you are most at risk of 'falling between the cracks' of society as your colleagues may shun you and the clinical autism system won't know what to do with you as it is geared towards those with 'obvious impairments'.

The 'Professional' autistic is part of the autism spectrum *least likely to obtain a clinical diagnosis* as you will often need to display 'obvious impairments' to get one (which is why research studies often show that most clinically diagnosed autistics are unemployed).

If you are working and living independently the diagnosing clinician may declare that you may be autistic but you 'do not need' a formal diagnosis as you are not displaying any 'obvious or severe impairments' or because you have developed your own coping mechanisms to adequately manage any traits causing you difficulty.

What the clinicians won't often understand is that in order to obtain your job and 'get by' in society you will have probably learnt to 'hide' or 'suppress' some of your more obvious behaviours or you will have trained yourself to communicate in the style and manner 'other people' use; they won't understand that you have requested an appointment to see them because this charade is *mentally and physically exhausting and about to burn you out.*

AM I AUTISTIC?

The successful professional autistic is most likely to be a workaholic because you are most likely to have the 'perfectionist' trait; that's why you're successful.

The 'workaholic perfectionist' style will come from the passion for getting your work 'right', but it might also be to compensate for your lack of skill in 'corporate politics'.

Due to the communication differences inherent with autistic people, the professional autistic is unlikely to be a natural at the social delicacies required to climb the 'promotion ladder' in the corporate workplace; the typical 'autistic style' of being too direct and too honest with no preference for idle small talk will not help you win friends and influence people in the corporate world.

As a result, if you are going to advance you might be aware that your work simply *needs to be better than anyone else's* because your social networking skills are unlikely to propel you forward.

I was recently told a story about a newly qualified autistic dentist who joined a practice in an area with a high immigrant population for whom English was not their first language so that this would minimise the need for small talk with patients.

What they hadn't considered was the small talk they would have to make with the staff.

This dentist then spent their lunchtimes 'hiding' behind the equipment in their clinic because the negative backbiting and sniping that took place in the staff room triggered off their *sensory overload* – the negative atmosphere literally overwhelmed their senses.

They then found an autism support group who helped them manage this scenario better.

In my case, when I graduated I got a decent job working for local government advising businesses on how to improve the fuel efficiency of their fleet.

I made the decision to leave within the year after I was informed by my manager that whilst my work was of a high standard I was 'working too quickly' and I should 'make my work last longer' as I was showing everybody else in the team up for their slow work rate.

Age 22 I then obtained a sought-after role at a large organisation which provided business advice and consultancy services; I was the youngest business advisor out of about 20 in the organisation and one of the youngest (if not the youngest) nationwide.

I was super-excited about this job as one of my special interests at the time was the 'business system' as I studied business at university (graduating with a 2:1) and was fascinated with the mechanics of business and how everything worked; I loved the idea of visiting different businesses each day and looking at ways to improve them.

Unfortunately there was a problem.

Unknown to me at the time I accepted the role there had been a huge internal dispute between the managers about whether I should be hired or not; two of them said 'yes', one of them said 'no'.

Unfortunately, the one who got overruled was my direct line manager; the one I was working with on a day-to-day basis.

And her uncle was the Chief Executive of the Organisation.

On my second day, as soon as we had our first 1-2-1 meeting she told me she didn't think I should have got the job (no reason given as to why). She made it clear she wanted me out of the job as soon as possible and was going to be 'watching my every move'.

I'm rather embarrassed to say that by lunchtime I was in floods of tears in the toilet.

My partner at the time and a friend were in the city centre that day and had dropped by to meet me for lunch expecting to hear about how exciting the new job was only to be rather surprised to find I was in a complete mess. Luckily, their moral support gave me the chance to get myself back together for the afternoon meetings.

I subsequently resolved to make sure I did the best work possible (which wasn't too hard as people rarely have issues with the quality of my work) and took great satisfaction from watching the 'horrible boss' come crawling up to me to offer her congratulations at the organisation's annual awards event after one of the businesses I was mentoring won a big award as a result of the application I researched and prepared on their behalf.

The Cloud In The Silver Lining

After that success 'the boss' took me out for a coffee so we could 'get to know one another better'.

My gut started churning; this type of cosy social *'chit chat'* with someone I vehemently didn't like just looked like a car crash waiting to happen.

Indeed, what this coffee meeting turned out to be was her 'bitching' in an incredibly unprofessional way about certain members of the team she was managing; mainly about their personal manner – nothing to do with their work – before trying to get me to agree and join her in criticising them by saying things like 'would you agree?' or 'had you noticed that?'.

Unfortunately for her (and me it would later turn out), there is a specific autistic trait that seems to prevent many of us from simply agreeing with what other people say; *if it's not true.*

This is a big issue in non-autistic corporate world where in order to advance it is usually very important you agree with everything 'the boss' says and that you don't point out any flaws in their view (there are some exceptions to this; some manager's encourage honest debate - but really they are the exceptions).

As a result the 'coffee shop chat' did not end well because I wouldn't join in with her bitching and so I then became 'Enemy No 1' (again) and had to leave the organisation a few months after that; not because there was any issue with my work but because this woman just made my life a living hell every single day.

This was my induction to the world of corporate politics.

After gaining a role as a Small Business Manager in a major bank age 23 I realised that I had developed a specific 'technique' for getting interviews (and jobs) often far above my age range and after I decided the corporate world was not for me I decided to use my 'technique' to help people who had a good skillset but lacked the social skills or application technique required to advance easily.

In 2004 I founded a career management agency which to date has built up a list of over 2,000 clients nationwide and as a 'Careers Expert' I have been asked to contribute to features in major newspapers and magazines many times throughout my career.

In the last 10 years' I have coached a *lot* of autistic trait clients in professional careers who all struggle with corporate politics, yet are clearly very talented at their work and I have devised a name for them;

The Invisible Autistic

The *Invisible Autistic* is often meticulous about their work and does very well up to a certain level but rarely progresses into the 'upper levels' of their workplace because the people at the top of the organisation tend to promote *people like them.*

If you are autistic in a non-autistic work environment you will often 'stand out' in some way and it is glaringly obvious that you are not *like them*. If you can't master the social nuances required to network with the managers; not just in the office but outside the office on the golf course, at their dinner parties or at 'after work drinks', you will hit a 'glass ceiling' at your workplace and find you are often congratulated on your work and yet frequently passed over for promotion.

This scenario can cause a huge amount of anxiety and frustration for the professional autistic and it can be difficult to understand why less talented colleagues are being promoted ahead of you.

To further compound matters, you may find yourself 'frozen out' by your colleagues (because you are not *like them*) and as a result find it difficult to make friends – potentially leading to social isolation, low self-esteem and in some extreme cases the development of depression.

In addition, if you are a workaholic perfectionist and are 'married to your job' you may not have met a romantic partner; further compounding the social isolation.

At work you are barely visible; in your personal life you might be *invisible.*

Contrary to the clinical research studies and media reports, I believe the professional autistic makes up the <u>majority of the autistic population;</u> they have to in some way because only a tiny proportion of adult autistics are diagnosed.

A sizeable proportion of the autistic population must be *employed* as those who are unemployed because their autistic traits are more 'obvious' are more likely to find themselves referred, clinically diagnosed and in receipt of disability/unemployment benefits than those who are in work and *seem* to have 'adapted well' or developed their own coping mechanisms.

The *invisible autistic* may have a nice job, nice house, one or two close friends and/or a partner and be perfectly happy. Like those other similarly happy, successful and *invisible* autistics over at Silicon Valley, the invisible autistic might not feel that they need a 'label'.

The clinicians would most likely agree – professional autistics are unlikely to get clinically diagnosed as autistic as it is unlikely they will display any *obvious impairments*; this is why it is easier for them to find work.

Invisible autistics can often be found working in specialist trades which require a high level of craftsmanship as well as the arts, the technology sector, academia, science, engineering, professional sports teams and any job which involves a specific talent or skill and a high level of attention to detail.

The invisible autistics are quietly making their contribution to society in huge numbers; but you'll never read about them in the news.

Don't Believe What You Read

Next time you read a negative story about autism being a 'burden to society' because '90% of autistics are unemployed' remember; that figure is taken from a tiny sample of <u>clinically diagnosed</u> autistic people.

As most adult autistics remain <u>undiagnosed</u> the **true figure** is more likely to be the other way round with most autistics *in work*; however the current clinical system has no way of recording this because they *cannot track the invisible autistics*.

How do I know that most autistics remain undiagnosed?

A) At 1-1.5% of the UK population, both clinical and charity data estimate that there are approx. 550,000 autistic *adults* in the UK (This figure has excluded 160,000 autistic children by using the same 23% aged under 18 rate as the rest of the population from data provided by the Office for National Statistics).

7

B) In July 2014, the *Cambridge Lifespan Asperger Syndrome Service (CLASS Clinic)* - which also calls itself the *'National Diagnostic Centre'* for autism - confirmed that it has diagnosed around **700 adults since the clinic was launched 15 years' prior**. That equates to approximately one diagnosis per week over the previous 15 years and is a tiny fraction of the overall adult autistic population (The CLASS Clinic is run by the same researchers who developed the AQ test covered in Chapter Five of this guide).

C) There are two other dedicated diagnostic centres in the UK with similar facilities. Due to NHS funding cuts they are log-jammed with extremely long wait times for a diagnosis. As a result it can be assumed that their rates will not be significantly higher than the CLASS clinic (which is also NHS-funded).

You don't need to be an autistic math genius to work out that once the 1/3 of adults with learning difficulties are removed from the 550,000 figure, even if the two remaining centres diagnosed *10 times as many* people as the CLASS clinic;

The vast majority of the adult autistic population are still undiagnosed.

The UK autism research organisation *'Autistica'* seems to confirm this view with their campaign for more research funding to help better diagnose autism and understand the lives of adult autistics; their official campaign brochure is entitled *'For the Hidden Half Million'*.

The Invisible Army: Where Are These Autistics?

The majority of autistic adults are undiagnosed most likely because they have a job, live independently and are able to 'get by' through hiding or working around some of their traits – or they are working in an environment supportive of their style (e.g. a software company or other technical role).

Autistics who are long-term unemployed and claiming benefits 'flag up on the system' and are more likely to get referred for a formal clinical diagnosis - *and be selected for research studies as a result* - than the invisible autistics who are working and 'getting by' and will *not show up on any system* or feature in any research studies or press stories.

Silicon Valley – The Original 'Invisible Autistics'

Silicon Valley has many examples of 'invisible autistics' in action.

Mainly because there is a whole area of California populated with them.

We all know that many of the social media gurus and whizz-kid programmers who work in that area have autistic traits; there's even a major cable TV show which makes fun of this 'autistic elephant in the room'.

Very aptly it's called *'Silicon Valley'*.

When I interviewed autistic agricultural scientist Dr. Temple Grandin (who designed more humane cattle handling facilities now used by 50% of cattle in the U.S) for *The Autism Issue (Temple Grandin on Autism, Innovation and the Secrets of Silicon Valley),* Dr. Grandin commented:

"The techies at Silicon Valley avoid the label…they totally avoid the label. I talked to a human resource person (from a well-known tech company) last year and she told me *'we know that they're probably Asperger's, but we don't talk about that'.*"

The world-changing innovation produced by the talented autistics in Silicon Valley will <u>never show up in any autism studies because they are not clinically diagnosed as autistic.</u>

These *invisible autistics* are in a supportive environment, happily working with other people like them and they are smart enough to know that in clinical terms autism is defined as a 'mental disorder'; they know they are not in any way 'mentally disordered' and they have no intention of being 'diagnosed' as such.

They don't want the label, they don't need the label and therefore they have no need for a diagnosis.

These are the original 'invisible autistics' and there are plenty more where they came from.

I Am An 'Invisible Autistic'

Even though I have authored this guide, I would not show up as being autistic on *any official records* or research studies on autism.

As a result, the fact I got my first job at 14 and always worked in retail or office jobs part-time around my studies at school and university, received high grades and have run businesses and ventures which have provided employment for many staff over the years would not show up in any research figures or media stories on autism.

And there are lots of other hard-working yet officially 'invisible' autistics like me.

What About The Research?

The CLASS clinic is run by the same team as the Autism Research Centre (ARC) and often provides the data which feeds into the ARC studies on autism which have made headlines in the press. Whilst ARC has conducted international research studies, the UK-based research taken exclusively from those diagnosed at the clinic has been sourced from a tiny sample of **700 clinically diagnosed autistics** who are more likely to display 'obvious or severe impairments' in order to meet the clinical diagnosis criteria.

The CLASS clinic data will never include the majority of invisible autistics who are working and contributing to society; either because they are reluctant to diagnose them because they don't show 'obvious or severe impairments' or because they simply never come into contact with them as the autistic is doing well and has no 'need' to see them.

This type of research has led to a fundamental misrepresentation of autistic people.

It is not the fault of the media but a damaging side-effect of a major flaw in the current clinical autism system for the reasons explained in the section outlining *'The Autism System'* covered in Chapter Seven of this guide.

The media are not autism specialists and therefore rely on the 'autism experts' for their information; they don't know any different.

It would be more accurate if the media reported the results of clinical research into autistic people as follows:

'This research is based on a small sample and may not be representative of the wider autistic population'.

If you find yourself following autism-related news stories more closely after reading this guide the above view might be a useful way to approach them.

Important Note: I use the term 'professional' autistic to distinguish between those who are *employed* and those who are *unemployed*; not as a description of personal character.

I believe those who are unemployed are under-served in the current clinical system and need more support to help them find work – most unemployed autistic people have very active minds and *want* to find work.

In contrast, whilst unemployed autistics may receive *some* support with social skills or finding work, it is important to highlight that the professional autistic receives *nothing* to help them navigate their way around the workplace or wider society; the professional autistic receives *no support at all.*

Some professional autistics in 'unfriendly' working environments struggle with anxiety and debilitating sensory overloads triggered by a stressful workload and exclusion from the 'social circle' at work. These autistics can be shunned by the clinicians who refuse to diagnose them and left to 'get by' *without any support.*

Whilst I have structured my own career around my preferred work environment, I still work alongside or coach other autistics in this situation and that is why I have drawn special attention to the plight of the professional autistic in this guide.

Chapter 2

WHAT IS AUTISM?

As a self-diagnosed autistic person who has read dozens of books on autism, discussed the topics covered in this book with many other autistic people and interviewed clinicians who specialise in researching or diagnosing autism both in the UK and the US, one thing is certain; *everyone has a different idea of what autism is.*

What do *you* think of when you think of autism?

• A heavily disabled child who doesn't speak?

• A child who has to wear one of those helmets because they are so hyperactive they keep running into walls?

• An autistic adult who lives with their parents being interviewed for something to do with autism on the news who speaks with a very monotonous tone?

• A gifted savant who can play a famous piano concerto by ear yet won't look anyone in the eye?

• Rain Man?

Here's what you might *not* think of straightaway when you think of autism:

• A 25 year old championship-winning pro surfer described by surfing legend Kelly Slater as "one of the best surfers in the world"

• A 26 year old American Idol Finalist who releases rock records and is married with a child

• Blue chip corporations implementing programmes to specifically recruit autistic IT specialists into their workforce in order to benefit from their autistic strengths

• An autistic person who doesn't speak yet communicates and has two-way conversations with people via assistive technology

• Autistic bankers, financial analysts, lawyers, scientists and doctors

• Autistic actors, ballet dancers and artists

• Autistic mechanics, welders and craftspeople

• Autistic pickers, packers and forklift truck drivers

• Autistic business owners

• An autistic woman

What do all of the above have in common? *They are all real examples of autistic people.*

Every single point on that list is a representation of a different part of the autistic spectrum from the hyperactive, head-banging autistic kid to the high-flying autistic analyst and the impeccably-balanced autistic ballet dancer.

If you are reading this guide I would guess it's because you have noticed (or it's been pointed out to you), that you have certain...*traits* which seem to annoy or confuse your colleagues/partners/friends/relatives/random people and stress you out.

At work, your colleagues might make jokes about your fastidious attention to detail and the way you might work longer and harder than they will to make everything more 'perfect' or to correct even the tiniest mistake you find in anything you are working on.

No-one understands why you are like this.

AM I AUTISTIC?

At social events you might seem to think differently to everyone else around you and you're never quite on the same 'wavelength' as the other people in the room. Sometimes you might find this quite tiring to the point where you would rather not socialise at all.

So what are the key autistic 'traits', do you have them and if so where do you sit on the autistic spectrum – if indeed you sit there at all?

Whilst a full list of the main autistic traits is covered in Chapter Four, below is a summary of the three key areas in which autistic people tend to differ from non-autistic people:

Communication Differences

• Autistic people tend not to be fond of 'superficial' small talk preferring to hold more in-depth conversations on a topic of interest.

• Ask an autistic person a direct question, and you will typically get a direct answer.

• Autistic people tend to prefer opinions to be backed up by quantifiable facts.

• Autistic people can have a rigid, unconfident or overly confident communication style which can mean that they can struggle in social situations and conventional job interviews.

Autistic Communication Differences: Job Interviews

Job interviews can be a challenging experience for an autistic person because they can say too much/too little and can often (but not always) stick to the rigid factual truth.

As Founder & Director of a Career Management Agency, I have worked with over 2,000 clients, with many of the clients who book me to help them prepare for interviews displaying prominent 'autistic traits'.

One of the key things an 'autistic trait' client will do when asked about their 'Strengths & Weaknesses' is be brutally honest about perceived weaknesses:

'I'm not a complete expert with xyz software'

'I don't have 100% knowledge of that particular market'

'Sometimes I find it difficult to bond with my colleagues'

What each of the above answers have in common, is that they are all *factually correct* but they are not what an employer wants to hear. The biggest challenge for me as a Career Consultant is re-training clients with autistic traits to always present themselves positively – whilst ensuring their answers remain truthful at all times as shown in my suggested answer below:

'I'm not a complete expert with xyz software – **but I am able to pick up new systems quite quickly with the proper training.'**

I usually get asked *'why do I have to change what I say?'* and I respond with an explanation of how interviews are like a 'game' and these are the rules of the game; if you don't play by them you simply get left behind and the person who interviews after you gets the job.

They understand this because this has already happened to them; they've been rejected for a job they know they are qualified for, had some bad feedback and find my agency.

Sometimes I use *'The interview is a stage and you have to give a performance'* analogy.

Either way, once the client understands one of these concepts the light bulb switches on and they want to know everything they can about the 'rules'. Once they understand the rules they start to adapt their answers in line with the rules and their interview performance (and confidence) suddenly gets a huge boost.

Why do the clients with autistic traits respond so well once the 'rules' are explained, and how am I as an autistic person able understand these 'rules' so clearly?

Preference For Order

Whilst I might describe the job-hunting/interview process as a 'game' (although certainly one with very serious consequences), what I am really interested in is not the 'game', but the rules behind it.

I am fascinated with all things business and one of my special interests is the job market including the different types of careers available, entry routes, salary levels, promotion opportunities and the actual nature of the job itself *(yes, autistic people have special interests – one cliché that is true. Although the same could be said about non-autistic people, autistic people often take their interests to another level).*

When I work with a client either writing CV's (or 'Resume's as you call them in the US!), delivering interview coaching sessions or providing career advice, I automatically absorb and remember every last detail about the roles the client has worked on or is interested in.

After 2,000 clients from all sectors in just about every job you can imagine (including newly-redundant Premiership Football Coaches, ex-Special Forces, chief executives, lawyers, nurses and tram drivers), I have an encyclopedic knowledge of potential adult career paths and the options available when a client has stumbled into one of the many pitfalls that can be encountered along the way…

The way I look at the job market matches one key trait of many autistic people; the ability to 'systemise'. The systemising trait is covered in more detail in Chapter Four, for the purposes of this summary it is described simply as a 'Preference for Order'.

In my case I look at the 'chaos' of the job-hunting process and identify the tried and tested techniques that work. Whilst some people see interviews as 'open-ended' explorations of a person's skills and experience, I see a closed, set structure with specific rules that if followed are likely to yield better results – whatever job you are interviewing for.

Push For Perfection

Many autistics are relentless perfectionists when working on a project they are interested in.

If you are reading this not as a potential autistic but as the *partner* of a person you think might be autistic, you will know that if your partner starts a project like redecorating the bathroom, it is unlikely they will leave it half-done.

The opposite is true.

It is likely they simply won't *rest* until it is completely finished and every tile has been slotted in as perfectly as possible. If there's a bit of grouting that hasn't been fitted properly, you might well find them ripping it all off and starting again until it fits perfectly.

At 2 'O' clock in the morning.

Obsession To Detail

Autistic people do tend to have a particularly obsessive attention to detail. No-one knows where it comes from, but it's definitely there. The level of attention to detail is generally precisely matched to the area of interest; a project/situation an autistic person is interested in will get an extraordinarily high level of attention to detail whilst a project/situation of no interest will most likely be met with apathy – but they may well highlight any perceived flaws in it anyway.

AM I AUTISTIC?

Sensory Differences

Some autistic people have likened being autistic to being on a different 'operating system' to non-autistic people; it could be said that autistic people are the MAC to the non-autistic PC.

Essentially, autistic people operate fundamentally differently to non-autistic people although we are all ultimately the same (a MAC and PC whilst different are both 'computers').

Both autistic advocates and non-autistic clinicians are agreed that autistic people experience the world differently. We have the same senses (sight, sound, touch, taste, smell) as non-autistic people, yet our senses often work differently.

Just as a MAC processes software differently to a PC (and still manages to run the programme), an autistic person processes their environment differently.

An autistic IT programmer might write a new computer algorithm in their mind before their fingers touch the keyboard.

An autistic musician might hear an entire arrangement for a new song before their hands touch a piano.

An autistic architect might walk by a plot of land and 'see' every last detail of the new building design in their mind before they put pen to paper.

Sensory Overload

What happens when you try and force a MAC to run software programmes designed for a PC?

It crashes.

In an autistic person with sensory sensitivities these 'crashes' can materialise in the form of a 'sensory overload' or 'meltdown'.

This is when the autistic brain suddenly starts working at the maximum capacity of its processing power trying to process an aspect of its environment that is alien, uncomfortable or just not the right 'fit'.

I just checked the task manager on my computer and the little green graph under the 'performance' tab shows that my computer is currently using just 1-6% of its processing power (or 'CPU' for those of you who are already looking up the performance of their computer).

As a result, my computer is running very quietly and making no noise. However, I do recall a time I installed a large, new piece of software and the fan on the computer started whirring manically as it tried to process all the new information being installed. Presumably at that time the CPU would have been close to 100%.

If you have ever seen the CPU of your computer hit 100% and stay at that level for any length of time then you know it will completely burn out, freeze, or just 'cut out'. Ultimately, it will stop working for a period of time and this is what can happen when an autistic person has a sensory overload.

This is not the 'fault' of the autistic person or any 'defect' with how the autistic brain is wired. Sensory overload will have triggered because the environment or an individual person (or persons') have tried to 'force' the autistic brain to process something it hasn't been built to process in that way.

It should be made clear that triggering a sensory overload (deliberate harassment aside), is rarely anyone's fault; the 'environment' can't help being noisy, the dog can't help barking and non-autistic people don't yet understand how the autistic brain works.

This guide covers more about sensory overload and how to better manage it in Chapter Four.

What Is Autism?

Most of the traits covered in this chapter can also be found in non-autistic people to varying degrees; you don't need to be autistic to be a perfectionist, not have a preference for small talk or have a preference for order and organisation (plenty of administrators with perfectly-organised filing cabinets can testify to that one!).

Differences in sensory processing go right down to the basic brain wiring of the autistic person and this is often the unique difference for many autistic people which leads autistic people to think and feel differently to non-autistic people.

So, What *Is* Autism?

A different way of thinking.

To paraphrase a well-known slogan from the company behind the MAC, autistic people simply 'think different'.

Chapter 3

AUTISM & THE AUTISM SPECTRUM

Readers' note: This section covers the origins of the current clinical view of autism. Those wishing to skip to the part which helps them find out whether they are autistic or not, please fast forward to the next chapter - 'A Guide to Autistic Traits'.

Those interested in finding out more about where the definition of autism came from, the concept of The Autism Spectrum and related debates, please read on.

*

At some point between 1908-10, Paul Eugen Bleuler a Swiss psychiatrist coined the term 'autism' from the Greek word 'autos' meaning self. The term was used to describe a person removed from social interaction; an isolated self.

In the 1940s Leo Kanner M.D. an Austria-Hungary born American child psychiatrist authored the research paper '*Autistic Disturbances of Affective Contact*'. This paper contained case studies of several children with limited speech and obsessive interests. Children with these traits were later defined as 'classically' autistic or 'Kanner's autistic'.

At the same time Kanner was exploring cases of primarily non-verbal autistic children, Austrian pediatrician Hans Asperger published the first definition of what later became known as 'Asperger's Syndrome'.

Asperger called this type of autistic child 'little professors' due to their ability to talk about their favourite subject in great depth and detail.

It has also been noted that Asperger himself seemed to exhibit strong autistic traits.

In the 1970s English psychiatrist Dr. Lorna Wing (who was herself mother to an autistic daughter), developed the concept of *'The Autism Spectrum'* and categorised autistic children into four groups broadly summarised as follows:

> • *The 'Aloof' Group* – These children will often be consumed with their special interests whilst seeming 'detached' and disinterested in their surroundings. This group was described by Dr. Wing as seeming to be 'in a world of their own'.

> • *The 'Passive' Group* – These children can be rather patronisingly called 'Autistic Angels' by their parents as they tend to be extremely obedient, well-behaved, intelligent and quiet.

> • *The 'Over-formal Stilted' Group* – These children are often very academically-minded and literal. This is the group who will often follow the Queen's English to the letter when they speak and may seem destined for Oxford/Cambridge/Ivy League universities.

> • *The 'Active but Odd' Group* – This rather controversial category is assigned to children who have full command of language, are extremely socially confident and energetic, yet tend to behave in what Dr. Wing has described as an 'odd' way. In her book *(The Autistic Spectrum: A Guide for Parents and Professionals 2003),* Dr. Wing highlighted that she had been searching for a more appropriate term for this group many years' but had never found one.

Sadly, Dr. Wing passed away a few months before this guide was written in 2014, before it could be suggested that a more appropriate term for this group could simply be *'The Extroverted Group'*. This is due to the other three categories being marked by introverted behaviours whereas this group has its distinction marked by an extroverted social confidence not typically displayed in the other categories.

The Autism Spectrum – An Autistic View

Dr. Wing coined the now largely defunct term 'Asperger Syndrome' in 1981 (the diagnosis of Asperger's was removed and merged into a broader 'Autism Spectrum' diagnosis in the fifth edition of the US-based Diagnostic and Statistical Manual of Mental Disorders in 2013). Whilst Dr. Wing should be commended for her work in highlighting that autistic people are part of a spectrum, autistic advocates (this author included) believe that autistic personalities are as varied as non-autistic personalities, autistic children develop differently as they mature into autistic adults and referring to the basic four category groups will risk re-enforcing narrow stereotypes of autism.

Whilst Dr. Wing took a pioneering approach with her view of *The Autism Spectrum* and the distinction between those who are autistic and those who are autistic with learning difficulties (the clinical view is that the majority – two-thirds – of autistic people *do not* have learning difficulties), unfortunately Dr. Wing also contributed to the proliferation of the reductive view of autism as a 'deficit' with her theory of autism as a '*Triad of Impairments*'.

The Camberwell Study – A New Theory Of Autism

In 1979, along with her colleague Dr. Judith Gould, Dr. Wing completed *'The Camberwell Study'*, an epidemiological survey of children living in the Camberwell area of London. From a population of 35,000 children, 914 children were selected for further study. These children were already known to the social, educational and health services and children were selected from the group if they had severe learning difficulties and/or if they showed one of the following: Social impairment, Verbal and non-verbal language impairment and Repetitive/stereotyped activities.

The additional screening resulted in the study focusing on a group of 132 children aged between 2 to 18 years who attended special schools.

The study found that *'all the children with social impairments had repetitive stereotyped behaviour and almost all had absence or abnormalities of language and symbolic activities. Thus the study showed a marked tendency for these problems to occur together'*.

By focusing on children in special schools already displaying 'impairments' in certain areas, this study gave rise to the concept of autism as a *'Triad of Impairments'* - a term devised and advocated by Dr. Wing and Dr. Gould.

Even though this 1979 study exclusively focused on *children with learning difficulties and/or impairments in special schools,* as a founding member of the *National Autistic Society (NAS* - the largest autism charity in the UK with close to 3,500 employees and nearly £100m in annual funding), Dr. Wing's 'autism as a deficit' theory of the *'Triad of Impairments'* subsequently became the widely-accepted view of both child *and* adult autism in the UK (and in the US up until the fifth edition of the DSM was released in 2013), and largely remains so to this day.

This theory still forms the basis of the *'What is Autism'* information for children and adults who think they may be autistic or have been recently diagnosed as autistic throughout the NAS website, the UK National Health Service (NHS) website and autism support group websites run by non-autistic parents across the UK.

Autism – The Autistic View

It is quite concerning that theories taken from the study of a small band of *children* in the 1940s/1970s remain the cornerstone of *adult* autism information and diagnosis 35-70 years' later.

AM I AUTISTIC?

Narrow 'impairment-only' views of autism completely disregard the true concept of autism as a spectrum which recognises that whilst some traits are impairments and create difficulties for the autistic person trying to live in a world not adapted to autistic people, some traits are clearly beneficial and of great advantage to the autistic person.

When you hear autism 'specialists' speaking in the media, they tend to describe autism as if it is *all* negative; as if there are no positives.

This narrow view is promoted by medical clinicians around the world and - as a consequence - the media and the general public seem to struggle to grasp the concept of the 'autistic individual', preferring instead to refer to extremely stereotypical and generic descriptions of 'autism' as if all autistic people are the same.

Whilst non-autistic people are aware that they may share *some* similar traits with their friends or work colleagues, it is taken for granted that they are recognised as having their own unique personality and they will expect to be treated as an individual - whereas autistic people are likely to find themselves having to fight for this basic 'right'.

Whose Spectrum Is It Anyway?

Clinicians talk about the concept of '*The Autism Spectrum*', but they don't really mean that in the true sense. When a clinician uses the phrase '*The Autism Spectrum*', what they are really talking about is 'The Autism *Impairment* Spectrum'; you can sit anywhere on it as long as you know that you have an '*impairment*' or three.

The clinical spectrum of autism does not recognise talents, gifts, special abilities, individual personalities or the 'right to be different' – it completely overlooks the contributions of autistic innovators, entertainers and artists to modern-day society and does not allow the ordinary autistic to just 'be' autistic; because to 'be' autistic is to not be 'normal' and to not be 'normal' is not acceptable to the medical profession.

Positive or neutral autistic traits simply <u>do not exist</u> in the clinical autism spectrum and this is why there is such a strong movement towards 'curing' autism in the US (less so currently in the UK) – many clinicians simply do not see any benefit at all to being autistic.

<u>In Summary</u>

Hopefully, this guide will help people who would like to read a more balanced and 'rounded' view of autism in contrast to the negative descriptions used by the clinicians in the media and in other autism books/guides.

In addition to helping you identify whether or not you may be autistic, this guide will cover the challenges of autism (because there are challenges) alongside the strengths and positives of autism in a way it would seem – only an autistic can.

As I am very certain that you, the reader would not want to be put in a 'personality box', or an 'impairment box', from this point on, when this author uses the phrase *'The Autism Spectrum'*, the meaning should be interpreted as an infinite combination of personalities and traits unique to each individual autistic person.

This surely is the true meaning of an autism *spectrum* after all.

Chapter 4

A GUIDE TO AUTISTIC TRAITS

The next few sections of this guide are designed to help you assess whether or not you or your family member/friend/partner/work colleague *might* be autistic. This section is designed as an overview/ reference guide to the main autistic traits. Have a read through and see if you recognise any of the traits; if you do it's time to check out the diagnostic tests available online which are covered in more detail in the next chapter.

*

Audio-Visual Synchronisation Differences

Some autistic people have difficulty processing simultaneous input from audio and visual channels. This has been described as watching a TV show with the sounds and images appearing to be 'out of sync' with one another and is thought to happen because the two senses send 'competing' instead of 'complimentary' information to the brain.

Some autistic people with audio-visual synchronisation difficulties prefer to watch TV with subtitles as this uses only one sense 'sight' as opposed to two senses 'sight and sound' so they find it easier to follow the story.

As it is not possible to 'add subtitles' during a social conversation (unless using sign language), this can cause problems with some autistics struggling to follow the flow of a conversation held in person as they find it difficult to simultaneously process the other person's body language/facial expressions as well as the content of what they are saying.

Conversely, once competing stimuli is removed autistics who previously struggled to process two senses at the same time can then display extremely sharp powers of observation or 'autistic perception' in the area they are strongest in (e.g. enhanced sight or sound sensitivities).

Attention To Detail/Perfectionism

Autistic people are often characterised by the way they pay attention to the tiniest of details. The benefits of this trait are that it is found in individuals at the highest levels of the science, engineering and creative sectors and this trait is extremely desirable to employers' recruiting for highly technical roles.

Recently, several large firms including SAP and Freddie Mac launched programmes specifically to recruit autistic people as software analysts due to their ability to spot tiny errors in large pieces of code.

The flip-side to this level of attention to detail is that sometimes autistic people can be extremely pedantic about details, much to the annoyance of friends, family members and colleagues as they can become so focused on 'details' that they sometimes don't see the big picture.

Related to the 'Attention to Detail' trait, Perfectionism in certain areas is often found with autistic people and again can lead to great success in their chosen field or area of interest. Conversely, the quest for perfection can lead to 'Perfectionist Anxiety' where an autistic person may not attempt to do a task unless they are certain they know exactly what to do and that they can do it perfectly.

Communication Differences

An overview of the key communication differences found with autistic people was covered in Chapter Two *(What is Autism?)*. A more detailed breakdown of typical communication differences can be found below:

• **Directness:** Autistic people are not generally keen on small talk on topics outside of their area of interest and may not see the point in saying ten words when one will do; some can be extremely direct in social and work conversations.

• **Social Faux Pas:** Autistic people can say things in a social setting that the prevailing culture dictates should typically be left unsaid.

• **Monologues:** One-way conversations which cover every detail of their special interest in great depth are common with some autistic people; this trait often improves with age as the autistic person gains greater social awareness.

• **Over-formality:** Some autistic people can have an extremely rigid communication style which makes them appear very formal and 'wooden' in social settings. This is a trait which is greatly misunderstood as non-autistic people can often misinterpret this formal manner as 'unfriendliness' and reject the autistic person without realising that this type of person, whilst not 'immediately' chatty may have layers of depth which reveal themselves over time.

• **Idioms and literal thinking:** Some autistic people interpet instructions and common turns of phrase literally. The phrase an 'eye-popping delight' used to describe a piece of art can cause distress in some who will take this phrase very literally. As they grow older and develop into adults, many autistics will 'learn' to understand the meaning of idioms.

Communication Differences & Social Exclusion

The above autistic communication differences are common causes of the 'rejection' of autistic people by non-autistic people both in the workplace and in social settings. This rejection can lead to difficulty making friends and social isolation follows as the autistic person finds themselves excluded from society or isolates themselves to avoid further rejection. This social exclusion can then lead to related and well-documented issues such as loneliness, anxiety and depression which are found in a disproportionately high percentage of the autistic population who haven't managed to successfully integrate themselves into mainstream society.

Communication Differences or Cultural Differences?

It could be said that a lot of the above communication differences are simply 'cultural' differences between autistic and non-autistic people. An autistic person with a preference for directness and formality is not suffering from an 'impairment' – they simply have a communication style which is in contrast to the dominant non-autistic culture. This difference then develops into an *impairment* only when it leads to social rejection and exclusion or makes it difficult to find work.

Difficulty Understanding The Concept Of Time

Some autistic people have immense difficulty developing a sense of time. This can materialise in different ways; they can have difficulty scheduling their workload, prioritising important tasks or may turn up for an event at the wrong time or on the wrong day.

There are now many useful strategies to help an autistic person structure their day/week including visual supports (e.g. a calendar with pictures of important tasks due that day), lists, colour coding of tasks and the use of mobile phones to store the times and dates of certain tasks/events.

Conversely, there have been (rare) documented incidences of autistics who can tell the time to the nearest minute without having a watch or any sight of a clock.

Distinctive Gait/Unusual Walk

Some autistic people have a very distinctive gait (walk) which involves walking in a very light 'bouncy' way, almost on tip toes.

Many autistic adults will have learnt to 'tone down' their walk following ridicule from fellow pupils in their school years', some however will retain this distinctive walk all their lives.

Echolalia

Whilst not unique to autism (it is also a key trait of Tourettes Syndrome), echolalia materialises in autistic people when a phrase or accent is repeated by the autistic person after they hear it on the TV/Radio or in overheard conversations; sometimes without any real understanding of what the phrase means or the context in which to say it.

In autistic adults without learning difficulties echolalia might seem to materialise in a conversation when they enthusiastically repeat a phrase said by the other person without actually responding to it or adding any further comment.

This is one of those more 'obvious' traits that most people will recognise as signalling that a person is autistic.

Excitability

One of the common autism traits is excitability/hyperexcitability. Whilst not present in all autistic adults, a significant proportion do display it. Excitability may materialise in the form of sudden 'energetic' behaviour which seems inappropriate or out of context to the situation at hand; for example bouts of sudden and unexpected laughter, a sudden display of impromptu gymnastics around the room or an overly enthusiastic response to incredibly trivial matters.

This behaviour whilst harmless in itself, can cause many issues for autistic adults. It can damage credibility in a work setting, deter prospective dates and lead to rejection from those who do not want to be associated with anyone displaying 'unusual' behaviour. Autistic excitability can also be a real danger to those who are more vulnerable and on an 'autistic high' as it can attract people seeking to exploit them whilst they are in this state.

Some scientific researchers are trying to find the cause of the electrical activity in the brain that triggers excitability in autistic people, so that they can find a drug which will suppress it.

Like many autistic traits it could be argued that this trait in itself is harmless to the autistic person – it is only ever the *response to the trait* from non-autistic people which deals the damage.

High Pitched Or Monotonous Tone Of Voice

Whilst most autistic adults speak 'normally', some speak with a high pitched melodic tone of voice or conversely an extremely flat, robot-like voice. Like most autistic traits, no-one really knows why this is but the end result is that the tone of voice is not likely to convey their feelings or emotions in a way that other people are likely to easily understand.

Whilst it seems to be incredibly difficult for behavioural therapists to alter this trait if present, many autistic children go on to develop a more varied tone of voice as they learn to emulate the traits of non-autistic people with age (this author included).

Literal Interpretations (Difficulty Understanding Idioms)

Some autistic people have a tendency towards 'literal thinking' or 'concrete thinking' which means that expressions/idioms like 'I've got a frog in my throat' can be extremely alarming for some, whilst an instruction to 'take a seat' can result in others physically picking up a seat.

This type of literal thinking can cause major issues in school/college or the workplace if teachers/managers think the autistic person is being sarcastic or ironic.

The irony is that literal thinking is classed as a 'communication deficit' and 'impairment' in autistic people by the medical profession who seem blissfully unaware that autistic people are simply interpreting and responding to language in the way it was originally intended to be used; it is other people who have subverted language with slang and banter away from its original meaning.

This is another trait which could be classed as a 'cultural difference' between autistic and non-autistic people as opposed to a 'deficit' or 'disorder' on the part of the autistic person.

Naivety

Some autistic adults can be very naïve. As a result they can be extremely trusting/unsuspicious of others, unsophisticated and lacking in worldly wisdom.

Whilst there is no explanation for this other than it is a trait possibly caused by delayed development and maturation (autistic people often retain certain 'childlike traits' for longer than non-autistic people), a clinician will say autistic people with this trait have a 'difficulty with perspective-taking'. In other words; they have a difficult time reading what another person might be thinking which means that they are slow to spot the malicious intentions of others.

This trait is extremely dangerous to autistic adults who have it as whilst they are viewed as 'adults' in the eyes of the law they can be easily led into participating in or admitting to criminal behaviour without realising the full consequences of their actions. As a result some studies are starting to look into the possibility that autistic adults can be led into providing false confessions by police, simply because they become very agreeable to whatever story the police are pressing upon them.

This 'childlike innocence' also makes both female and male autistics of all ages at particularly high risk of falling victim to sexual predators and/or physical assault.

Unfortunately, autistic adults only seem to learn to manage this trait following a bad experience and even then usually only by isolating themselves from wider society and adopting a reclusive lifestyle.

Reclusiveness

Not all autistics are reclusive, however there are many who remain on the 'fringes' of mainstream society.

Some may be reclusive not by choice but because they have found themselves socially excluded by the non-autistic society they live in.

Some may simply have a preference for solitude and have made a conscious decision to remain socially isolated or hermit-like because it suits them; they may simply find it too exhausting being in a cultural environment which is not tailored to them and so 'live in their own world' instead.

It is often said that many autistic people have just one friend because that's all they need. As long as they have that one person (or partner) they don't need anyone else as they don't need extended levels of social contact; they would prefer to keep themselves occupied with their special interests instead.

It should be made clear that whilst 'selective reclusiveness' is relatively common with autistic people, there are many autistics who have great difficulty interacting with other people due to the traits listed in this guide and the enforced social isolation creates additional issues such as depression and anxiety.

Equally, there are many autistic people who have integrated well into their workplace or social group because they work around like-minded people or have a shared interest which they can discuss at length with their friends. These could be considered the 'invisible autistics' who don't feel the need to go for a formal diagnosis and so never come into contact with the clinical sector and as a consequence don't show up in any research studies on autism.

As mentioned earlier, the most well-known group of 'invisible autistics' live in Silicon Valley. They are the autistic 'geeks' who work as programmers for the big technology companies without the word 'autistic' ever being mentioned.

These autistics are very talented, have sustained employment and develop a strong social circle of people like them. As a result they do not often run into the 'challenges' that many out of work autistics do; until they step outside of their social circle.

These autistics and others like them provide fuel for the view that autism in its natural environment is not a 'disorder'. In otherwise healthy autistics, autism only becomes a 'disorder' when it is forced to comply with the 'norms' and behaviours of a non-autistic society.

Routines/Repetition/Rituals

Many autistic people have a strong preference for routines and a set structure in their life. It is not known why autistic people tend to prefer order, structure and predictability but it is known that some autistics can get very distressed if their daily routine is altered or disrupted in any way.

Routines and rituals can cover anything in the life of the autistic person including food, clothes, activities and household objects. Routines can include eating exactly the same food at the exactly same time every day, wearing the same clothes every day (or different clothes which are identical), going for a walk or exercising at the same time every day or insisting that certain brands of household products/toiletries are purchased.

Those with a preference for routine will benefit from working in a job which follows exactly the same routine or ritual every day. Conversely, any changes to a job or the environment the autistic is working in – however small – can cause high levels of anxiety and irritation.

Repetitive behaviour in adult autistics is a physical behaviour which might involve lining up objects in a certain order or the repetitive use of an object e.g. repeatedly flicking a rubber band.

Lining up of objects (e.g. categorising books by height order on a book shelf) can be linked to systemising or the 'preference for order', whilst repetitive 'playing' with an object can often be soothing to autistics and helps reduce anxiety.

Whilst many adult autistics will learn to regulate this type of behaviour around others as they mature, some may visibly revert back to it when under extreme stress.

Selective Mutism

Whilst selective mutism is not an 'autistic trait' per se (as you can be selectively mute without being autistic), in autistics this trait is often caused by sensory overload and frequently occurs when child and adult autistics have a 'meltdown' and so is included in this guide.

With selective mutism the autistic adult 'shuts down' and becomes mute when they are experiencing a sensory overload triggered by high levels of stress or anxiety.

The main difference between non-autistic children (and it is mainly children) and autistics who are selectively mute is that with non-autistic children:

A) It's more common in girls and children of ethnic minority populations who have recently migrated from their country of birth.

B) More than 90% of children with selective mutism also have a social phobia or social anxiety.

C) They often grow out of it with age.

D) It mainly appears in unfamiliar environments outside of the home.

E) Non-autistic children tend to respond to behaviour therapy as the therapy focuses on reducing the anxiety which triggers the mutism.

In contrast, when autistic children and adults experience selective mutism it has no relation to the cultural background of the autistic, will activate both inside or outside the home in familiar and unfamiliar environments, doesn't respond well to therapy and when the children grow into adults the trait can still remain; even an accomplished adult autistic can be rendered mute when sensory overload strikes.

Sensory Differences

As discussed previously in *Chapter Two; What is Autism?*, autistic people experience the world differently. Whilst autistic people have the same senses as non-autistic people, their senses can often work differently leading them to process their environment differently.

This is a key difference between autistic and non-autistic people.

Autism and 'eccentricity' often get confused with wives sometimes volunteering their husbands as being a 'bit autistic' because they display some peculiar behavioural traits.

Whilst debate continues around *'What is Autism'*, which traits are uniquely autistic and which traits are simply more common in autistic people; certain sensory differences in brain wiring do seem to be exclusive and unique to autistic people and should not be confused with an 'eccentric manner'.

Sensory differences can materialise in the form of over-sensitivity (hypersensitivity) or under-sensitivity (hyposensitivity) in certain areas which are summarised below along with examples of how different sensory perception can be a real strength to the autistic person – as opposed to the clinical view of these differences being solely a 'disorder' or 'deficit'.

Sight

Hypersensitivity to light can cause distorted vision and cause images to blur whilst *hyposensitivity* can cause objects to appear darker than they are or cause difficulties with depth perception.

> • **The Autistic Advantage:** An autistic person who benefits from hypersensitive pin-sharp sight without any distortion can make an expert sportsperson and some autistic people have expert depth perception and make brilliant architects or artists. Equally, the autistic with distorted vision or differences in depth perception can create distinctive artwork as has been the case with blind or partially-sighted autistic artists like Richard Wawro.

Visual Thinking

Some autistics (this author included) use their 'sight' sense differently and 'think in pictures'.

Autistic scientist and author Dr. Temple Grandin explains this in great detail in her talks and books and has previously commented that she is able to *"translate both spoken and written words into full-color movies, complete with sound" and that "Visual thinking has enabled me to build entire systems in my imagination" ('Thinking in Pictures', Temple Grandin, 2006).*

This unique way of thinking has enabled Dr. Grandin to achieve huge success with her work as an equipment designer in the agricultural industry.

Sound

Autistic people who are *hypersensitive* to sound might find that sounds become magnified or distorted and they may experience an inability to filter background noise which leads to difficulty concentrating on work, study or conversations. Some autistics with very sensitive hearing can hear conversations from some distance away.

Hyposensitivity to sound may result in partial hearing, a lack of response to certain sounds or a preference for loud, noisy environments like racetracks or train stations. Autistics with this trait may also enjoy banging or shaking objects to hear a certain sound.

> • **The Autistic Advantage:** Some autistics with sound sensitivities are known for having 'perfect pitch' when they sing, play or write music.

Touch

Hypersensitivity to touch can be extremely unpleasant for an autistic person who might find even the lightest touch uncomfortable at best, painful at worst. Clothing can also be an issue as it can feel scratchy and uncomfortable to some. Most autistic adults are aware of their sensitivities and will wear only what they feel comfortable in.

Hyposensitivity to touch may result in a dangerously high pain threshold which can cause issues if the adult doesn't feel their body telling them when something is causing pain e.g. when a bath is too hot.

• **The Autistic Advantage:** Autistics who are under-sensitive to touch and have a strong body awareness can excel in physical sports and activities as well as jobs which involve all-weather 'outdoor' work.

Taste

Hypersensitivity to food can result in a restricted diet as the autistic has very sensitive taste buds and will find that eating many 'strongly flavoured' foods will provoke an intense reaction. In addition to the taste of food, certain autistics can be sensitive to textures and will prefer 'soft' or 'smooth' foods like mashed potatoes, jelly or ice cream.

Hyposensitivity to taste will often include a preference for very strongly flavoured/spicy foods.

• **The Autistic Advantage:** Hypersensitivity to food can lead certain autistics to be very successful in the catering or food technology sector; particularly in the area of food or wine tasting.

Smell

An autistic person with *hypersensitivity* to smell can find strong smells intense and overpowering. In autistic adults a sensitivity to smell can be triggered by a wide range of scenarios including being in a lift with someone with a distinctive perfume or walking past the bins awaiting collection on 'bin day'.

An autistic person with *hyposensitivity* to smell might have almost no sense of smell at all and this can result in a failure to notice extreme odours including their own body odour. Some autistic people with a hyposensitivity to smell may lick food items instead of smelling them to get an idea of whether they are still good to eat or not.

• **The Autistic Advantage:** An autistic person with a keen sense of smell who enjoys certain fragrancies might be found in the cosmetics sector formulating new fragrancies for products like shampoo or body lotion. They could also make excellent perfumiers.

Balance

An autistic person with a *hypersensitive* vestibular (balance) system may find it difficult to co-ordinate their movements which causes difficulties with walking down the street or sporting activities. They may also experience motion sickness.

An autistic person with a *hyposensitive* vestibular system may find it difficult to assess their own sense of balance and may need to rock, swing or spin to gain a sense of how they are positioned.

• **The Autistic Advantage:** Autistics with a hypersensitive and correctly aligned sense of balance may be found in the top tiers of professions/sporting activities which require precision-balance including ballet, dance, gymnastics, martial arts, surfing and equestrian activities.

Body Awareness

Body awareness (proprioception) is to do with the sense of 'personal space' and is a common autistic sensitivity.

An autistic person who has *hypersensitive* body awareness is likely to be incredibly sensitive to anyone venturing into their 'personal space' and may react strongly if their personal boundaries are breached. Common 'space breaches' for autistic adults might involve walking down a crowded street, being jostled by other passengers on public transport or working in an office environment where the person next to them is sat 'too close'.

43

Conversely, *hyposensitive* body awareness can result in the autistic person breaching the personal space of others by inadvertently standing too close or accidently bumping into people as they cannot effectively measure their proximity to other people. They may also find it hard to navigate rooms without bumping into things.

> • **The Autistic Advantage:** Similar to those with a strong sense of balance, autistics with a strong sense of body awareness will often excel in roles which require physical precision including sports and the arts.

Sensory Overload/Meltdowns

Whilst every autistic person is different and will have different sensory sensitivities, autistic people do seem to have one thing in common; often they will have experienced a sensory overload at some point in their life.

Sensory overloads (or 'meltdowns' to give them their popular term) are triggered when one or more senses that the autistic is sensitive to get overloaded with sensory input e.g. an autistic with noise sensitivities might have a meltdown triggered by the siren on an emergency vehicle. As the autistic brain is wired differently to non-autistic brains, the day-to-day sensory sensitivity of an autistic can be a more intense experience than the day-to-day world of the non-autistic.

No two sensory overloads are the same and every autistic experiences them differently, however there are common themes including a feeling like the 'brain is on fire' or 'ice picks in the brain' when one is triggered.

When an extreme overload is triggered the autistic adult may fly into a state of panic or anger or just 'shut down' completely – like a statue.

Although a lot of emphasis is put on the *autistic* meltdown, it should be remembered that non-autistic people have meltdowns too; they just display them differently.

One key difference between the autistic meltdown and the non-autistic meltdown is that the non-autistic is often aware that they are causing a scene and has the option to take it 'behind closed doors' if they choose to.

In contrast, the autistic will have one wherever it triggers and may be not be aware of what is happening around them; in the case of an extreme overload some may lose all sense of where they are at that point in time.

How To Avoid A Meltdown

Any autistic (and those who witness one having a meltdown) will tell you that sensory overload is very difficult to 'manage' once it begins and that even though it may last just a few seconds or minutes until it 'burns itself out', a meltdown is an extremely distressing experience which can take the autistic hours, days or weeks to recover from.

As a result, age and maturity generally teaches adult autistics that meltdowns need to be *avoided* at all costs.

Self-aware adult autistics will often have learnt to spot when one is developing and quickly exit the scenario. They will also likely take care to avoid scenarios where one is likely to develop e.g. they will stop going to the cinema if they know the bright screen and noise is likely to trigger a sensory overload.

Some autistics find that regular practice of common relaxation techniques such as mediation or yoga – or even just setting time aside to listen to their favourite (calming) music once a day can help reduce their overall stress levels and as a consequence provide them with an improved alertness of when overload is developing, along with more 'bandwith' to prevent an overload once they can feel it starting to develop.

If you are reading this guide because you think there is a chance you may be autistic and you don't recognise any of these sensory differences and have never experienced sensory overloads or 'meltdowns' in the way described above; it could be considered *unlikely* you are autistic.

Special Interests

Many autistic people have special interests in a particular area with the range of potential interests limitless and too numerous to list in this guide. Autistic special interests provide a space for the autistic to lose themselves in their own world and if these interests are in an area which has a practical application in the workplace (e.g. IT, science, engineering or the creative sector), the autistic who finds work in their area of interest will almost certainly be one of the most knowledgeable and skilled employees in the organisation as they won't switch off when 'work' finishes; they will keep working on the project long after everyone else has gone home because they want to 'perfect' their knowledge or skill in that particular area.

One of the issues with the autistic adult 'special interest' is that it doesn't always have an obvious practical application in the workplace (e.g. collecting DVD's or playing video games), and if the autistic is dedicating all of their focus in one narrow area of interest it can tip the 'interest' into an 'obsession'. This is best seen in the numerous cases of autistic adults who are obsessed with video games and will sit and play for 12+ hour sessions without a break, without food and without any awareness of or interest in what is happening in the house/world beyond the TV screen.

There is much debate as to where parents supporting unemployed autistic adults should 'draw the line' between encouraging a special interest as a way to connect and bond with their child and where to discourage the interest in the hope their child will better integrate with society.

Only one thing is certain; completely cutting off access to a special interest will likely be highly distressing to the autistic adult.

Stimming

Self-stimulatory behaviour (also known as stimming and self-stimulation), is the repetition of physical movements and/or sounds, or the repetitive movement of objects and is a very distinctive autistic trait; although not all autistics will display it.

The more 'obvious' cases of stimming in adults might involve body rocking, hand-flapping and repeated touching or stroking of certain fabrics or textures.

Whilst there is a lot of debate as to why these behaviours arise, a commonly accepted view is that stimming utilises the different sensory processes of the autistic person and is used as a way to relieve negative emotions or experience 'pleasant' feelings.

Whilst stimming is a very soothing behaviour and commonly seen in autistic children, by the time an autistic person reaches adulthood many will have grown out of their childhood behaviours or learnt to hide or minimise their use of stimming from public view.

Aside from the self-injurious forms of stimming including head-banging and repeated scratching/rubbing, most stimming behaviours are harmless. However despite this, there is an industry of 'therapists' and pharmaceutical companies trying their best to eliminate these behaviours through drugs or behavioural therapy.

Systemising

This trait has an expanded section as along with Communication Differences and Sensory Differences it is a key autistic trait.

Systemising is the drive to analyse or construct a system with a system being anything that follows rules and/or laws. A system can be mechanical (e.g. a car), abstract (e.g. number patterns), natural (e.g. the weather) or collectible (e.g. cataloguing of DVDs by name).

It is possible that autistic people tend to 'systemise' better than non-autistic people due to (amongst other things), their attention to detail and preference for order.

When an autistic person has a 'special interest' often it will be a form of systemising. If they are transfixed by following the flow of water in a stream it could be because they want to understand what makes the water flow in one direction, what makes it flow at all or why some parts of the water look brighter (due to reflected sunlight) than others.

One systemising-related trait common in autistic people is 'bottom-up thinking'. Whereas academics tend to take a 'top-down' view by stating a hypothesis that *this* is like *that* because of *this* before trying to find evidence to support their view, autistic people tend to look at the available evidence *first*, spot any obvious patterns or trends and then form a view from that – they would be unlikely to start with a pre-formed view.

An example would be that if presented with just one piece of a puzzle a non-autistic academic would be likely to 'guess' at what shape or form the rest of the puzzle is likely to take and then look for other pieces of a puzzle which match that shape to fit that view. An autistic person presented with just one piece of a puzzle is likely to either shrug their shoulders and say 'I don't know' when asked what the rest of the puzzle may look like (often incorrectly labelled as a 'lack of imagination'), or make finding the rest of the puzzle their 'special interest' and spend hours searching for all available puzzle pieces. They would then only form an opinion once every single puzzle piece had slotted together perfectly – they will not tolerate a missing piece of the puzzle.

The advantages of the autistic who thinks in this way is that when they have formed an opinion you can be sure they will have analysed every possible piece of research/evidence available and used their attention to detail to spot trends and patterns in the data that others might struggle to see.

The downside is that academics use hypotheses for a reason; to narrow down their research into one workable area. This is also why polling companies use small samples of the population to try and guess voter preferences across the whole country as trying to canvass the views of the entire population is expensive, exhausting and often impossible. Of course, the inherent flaw with 'small-sample thinking' is that it often leads to incorrect results.

During the 2014 vote on Scottish Independence, the Canadian polling company hired by the Scottish National Party were so confident of a 'YES' vote based on their small-sample research that they released their 'YES' prediction to the press *before the votes were counted.* This apparently encouraged the 'YES' camp to contact journalists and advise of a planned victory speech; before the actual results were announced and crushing defeat loomed.

It could be said that an 'autistic thinker' would never feel confident in the results of a 'small-sample' poll or piece of research as there would be too many 'missing pieces of the puzzle' to draw a convincing conclusion.

The Autistic Need For A Complete Picture – An Autistic View

The practice of researching a tiny sample of the population and forming an opinion on the wider population based on the initial sample has limited value in the view of this author.

Along with much published 'research' it should have the disclaimer of 'taken from a small sample of the population therefore actual results may vary'. Whilst interesting from an anecdotal point of view, sample-based research - which is the basis of all available research

<u>on autism</u> - is invariably formed from simply too small a sample to provide anything close to absolute accuracy.

As highlighted in *Chapter Two; What is Autism?* - some of the most widely-accepted research on autism has been taken from pools of just 10-140 autistic children in the 1940s and 1970s and has been subsequently extrapolated to the rest of the autistic population – including adults – and remains in use 40-80 years' later with modern researchers seeming to forget that the original research is based on a hypothesis – a *guesstimate* of what autism is; not actual fact.

This is why autism is still characterised as a 'disorder', a 'triad of impairments' or a 'disease' which needs curing.

Sample-based research is why autism is so misunderstood; the main theories have been devised by non-autistic clinicians with a 'top-down' approach – they form a pre-set idea of what autism is (a set of specific impairments for example) and then look for evidence to match their hypothesis by *screening out* those who don't fit their hypothesis from the initial sample.

Autism research as it stands today has been based on only *one piece of the puzzle* with researchers simply guessing at what the rest of the puzzle looks like.

To contrast, a systemising-oriented autistic with a special interest in autism research is unlikely to rest until data or observations from the entire population have been collected on that particular topic.

Once they have collected all available information they will be able to spot patterns and trends in the data and be confident in stating a more comprehensive and conclusive finding than would be generated from 'small-sample' research.

Of course, this interest can turn into an 'obsession' with the autistic systemiser unable to switch off until they have collected all available information on the topic - even if it takes the course of their entire lifetime; and this is where the line between 'madness' and 'genius' can start to get blurred.

Analysing VS. Creating Systems

Some autistics like creating systems whilst other autistics are content with just analysing their system of interest; once they have fitted all the pieces of the puzzle together they might lose interest, or they might want to do it all over again with a different puzzle.

Some autistics are only interested in fitting together the pieces of the puzzle perfectly so that they can learn to create a 'perfect' puzzle of their own. This trait is found in those who come up with innovative and creative new ways of doing things; programmers who work around-the clock designing ground-breaking new computer programmes, architects who design innovative energy-efficient buildings and concert pianists who create intricate original pieces.

In Summary

Not every autistic is a relentless systemiser and often this trait is misunderstood in those who are; for example when a child who is fascinated with watching rain is criticised as 'staring out the window' or having a 'pointless interest', when actually they are analysing why rain falls, what makes rain, why are some raindrops bigger than others ect.

The systemising autistic won't want to be *told* what rain is; they will like to work things out for themselves and in doing so they might just spot a tiny detail in the way rain falls that everyone else has missed...

The Next Step To Self-Diagnosis

By now you should have a good idea of whether or not you or your partner/friend/relative/colleague may be autistic; however this is only the first part to self-diagnosis. Part two starts in the next section which explores the online autism diagnostic tools available. If you think there is a chance you might be autistic – it might be time to venture online and complete these tests for further exploration.

Chapter 5

A GUIDE TO THE ONLINE AUTISM DIAGNOSTIC TESTS

Over the next few pages this guide will explore three of the most common online autism tests. Assuming you have read through the traits in the previous section you should already have an idea of whether or not you or your partner/family member/friend sit somewhere on the autism spectrum.

For those who think they may be autistic, this next step is about exploring where you may sit on the spectrum.

The tests covered in this section are not designed to provide you with a full, formal diagnosis as currently this can only be done by a medical practitioner.

However, they are very useful for those who do not want/need to visit a clinician and would instead like to know for their own information whether or not they may be autistic; this is what 'self-diagnosis' is.

The tests covered in this section are as follows:

- The AQ (Autism-Spectrum Quotient) Test

- The SQ-R (Systemising Quotient Revised) Test

- The Aspie Quiz (Final Version 3)

About The Tests

This guide covers the most widely-used autism and autism-related tests currently available. There are other tests available which may be covered in future editions of this guide when their use is more widespread and more evidence is available to support the validity of them.

The AQ test tends to be used in conjunction with the Empathy Quotient (EQ) test in a clinical setting. Chapter Eight covers more about the EQ test and why it hasn't been included in this section.

Find These Tests At AmIAutistic.com

As these tests tend to be hosted by third party commercial sites who can change/remove links to the tests at any time, this guide doesn't link to them directly and instead has an accompanying webpage at www.amiautistic.com/tests - please visit this page to find the latest links to these tests.

THE AUTISM-SPECTRUM QUOTIENT (AQ) TEST

Find a link to this test at www.amiautistic.com/tests

• Number of Questions: 50

• Approx. Time Taken: 10 minutes

About

Devised by the Autism Research Centre in Cambridge, UK the test covers five different fields the test developers associated with the autism spectrum: social skills, communication skills, imagination, attention to detail and attention switching/tolerance of change.

The initial trial of this test showed that the average non-autistic score is 16.4 (out of 50) with **80% of adults diagnosed as autistic scoring 32 or more**. The developers of the test cite a score of 32 or more as indicating *"clinically significant levels of autistic traits"*.

Pros

• A 'Clinical Standard' screening test used in a variety of clinical and healthcare settings in the UK.

• The test is a commonly-used tool for self-diagnosis.

• The test has been clinically tested for consistency.

• Simple 'single score' results mechanism makes it easy to identify where you sit on the 'AQ scale'.

• The test is a good starting point for exploring where you might sit on the *clinical* autism spectrum.

• The test is a well-recognised discussion point for people who might want to discuss their results on forums or at adult autism support groups.

Cons

• The questions can be quite challenging to complete.

• The test is not particularly useful if you score in the 'mid-range'.

• The AQ has been devised by clinicians and therefore is biased to their clinical view of what autism is.

• This tool is not widely used in clinical settings in the US.

AQ Test Summary

Although the test is titled *'Autism-Spectrum Quotient'*, the single score results mechanism delivers results on a narrow, linear scale rather than a 'spectrum' in the way that the *Aspie Quiz* does.

As a consequence the results lack depth and fail to provide any insight into the takers' specific autistic traits or their place on the wider autism spectrum.

However, as the 'AQ score' is easily recognisable to other self-diagnosed and clinically diagnosed autistics, it is still a useful reference point for debates on forums and at support groups for where you sit on the 'scale'.

In addition, as the AQ test can be used in a clinical setting for autism screening ahead of a formal diagnosis in the UK, knowledge of where you sit on the scale is essential for those seeking a formal diagnosis.

AM I AUTISTIC?

SYSTEMISING QUOTIENT-REVISED (SQ-R) TEST

Find a link to this test at www.amiautistic.com/tests

• Number of Questions: 75

• Approx. Time Taken: 15 minutes

About

The SQ-R test is developed by the same team who developed the AQ test and is based on the premise that systemising is the drive to understand, construct, predict and/or control the rules of a system. As this is something autistic people seem to be particularly interested in, one of the aims of this test is to identify the extent of 'systemising traits' with the initial clinical study of this test showing an average non-autistic score of 55.6 (out of 150) and an average autistic score of 77.2.

Pros

• The questions are relatively straightforward to complete.

• The test has been clinically tested for consistency.

• Simple 'single score' results mechanism makes it easy to identify where you sit on the 'SQ-R scale'.

Cons

• The SQ-R has been accused of being used by the test developers to find evidence to support a contested gender-biased theory of autism and is therefore somewhat biased to the developers clinical view of this subject.

• The SQ-R isn't as widely used as the AQ test or Aspie Quiz and on its own it does not make for a particularly useful reference point when discussing autistic traits with other autistics in forums or at support groups.

SQ-R Test Summary

This test is a revised version of the SQ test and even though the test has been revised due to claims the questions on the original SQ test had a 'male gender bias', there are still some unresolved issues with the gender-based theory behind the SQ-R test.

Setting the controversial theory behind the test aside, when taken in conjunction with the other tests in this guide, the SQ-R can provide a useful insight into the taker's tendency towards a 'systemising brain' (as opposed to the 'extreme male brain' theory linked to the test). As a result the SQ-R can be a useful - though not essential - additional step towards the 'self-diagnosis' process.

AM I AUTISTIC?

THE ASPIE QUIZ (FINAL VERSION 3)

Find a link to this test at www.amiautistic.com/tests

• Number of Questions: 150

• Approx. Time Taken: 20-30 minutes

About

The original version of this test was developed by a small team of independent researchers with the aim of checking for neurodiverse / neurotypical traits in adults; as described at the start of the test page. 'Neurodiverse' is the developers preferred name for Asperger's or 'Aspie's' as the test refers to them, with 'Neurotypical' being the name for non-autistic people.

This test has been through several revisions over the years with the current version *'modified to catch more of the relationship issues'* according to the developer. The test now covers the following areas; *talent, perception, communication, social, contact and attachment* in both autistic and non-autistic contexts.

Pros

• The test is extremely comprehensive and produces a PDF report of the results which includes a very useful illustrative diagram (better known as the 'Spider Diagram') of where the taker sits on the spectrum in the areas measured.

• This test is great fun to take with both autistic and non-autistic partners/friends/family members to see where you both 'sit on the spectrum' and debate the differences in your results.

• The taker's 'Spider Diagram' is often shared on autism forums and results have been shown to consistently differ vastly from one autistic person to another making the test a good way to help people understand that autism is not linear in the way the AQ test implies and is instead a spectrum with every autistic person occupying their unique and distinctive space within it.

• This seems to be the most popular test within the autistic community and as a result the 'Aspie Quiz Score' is easily understood with the taker's 'Spider Diagram' often shared online as a good starting point for discussions about their traits on forums and support groups.

• This test has been devised by a researcher who identifies as 'neurodiverse', which might explain why the test connects well with the autistic community.

Cons

• As it is so comprehensive it does take longer to complete than the other tests.

• Whilst the test seems to have been originally devised by a team of two, it now seems to be run by one developer who is using data from the results to explore his personal research into 'the function and evolution of neurodiversity'. As a result there are some 'required' questions on blood type and other personal specifications at the start of the test alongside some peculiar questions that seem related to evolutionary traits within the test – although apparently these have no bearing on the outcome of the test; they are there to help the researcher gather information for his theory.

The Aspie Quiz (Final Version 3) Summary

'Final Version 3' launched in 2014 and previous versions of this test have tended to be the most popular choice of test within the autistic community as the results provide more depth and insight into where the taker sits on the 'spectrum' in the true sense of the word.

Chapter 6

HOW YOUR CHILDHOOD TRAITS WILL HELP TO TELL YOU IF YOU ARE AUTISTIC

If you ever go for a formal autism diagnosis as an adult you will find that the clinician will pay a lot of attention to your background growing up and they will often want you to bring a parent, sibling or guardian who can provide them with information on your behaviour as a child. This is because as an adult new behaviours can be learned and some old behaviours un-learned.

A lot of adults requesting a formal autism diagnosis from a clinician will do so in a state of distress; possibly because they are finding it difficult to manage certain traits, to establish a fulfilling social life, find work or meet a partner and they think this *might be* because they are possibly autistic.

When conducting the diagnosis a clinician will want to know if the presenting 'symptoms' are due to nature or nurture; e.g. is this person presenting these issues because they *are* autistic or because this happens to be the situation they have found themselves in and someone has suggested it might be because they are *possibly* autistic.

As you can't tell whether or not someone is autistic just by looking at them, one of the best ways to identify whether an adult *is* autistic is by examining their childhood traits; if they are autistic they will have displayed specific traits in childhood which they won't have learnt to hide or manage with age. Conversely, if someone is *not autistic* but has developed some autistic-like traits with age the clinician would expect nothing unusual to display in their childhood traits.

One of the issues with the online diagnostic tools is that you are answering them as an adult who has most likely learnt to adapt some of your behaviours.

In the case of this author, I know some of the questions I answered recently related to traits I have learnt to manage or minimise with age and so my answer would make it seem as if a trait which was very pronounced when I was younger is now 'not present' – yet if I had completed the test based on my 12 year old self I would have scored *far higher* than I do already (and I already score reasonably high - but more on that in the next chapter).

As a result, no autism self-diagnosis is complete without an assessment of your childhood traits.

How To Assess Your Childhood Traits

For those of you reluctant to visit a clinician with a relative and go over every aspect of your developmental years, a good way to identify whether or not you had any autistic traits in childhood from the comfort of your own home is simply to go through the traits outlined in *Chapter Four* of this guide with a parent, relative or guardian and ask them to highlight any traits you displayed as a child.

By this point, you may well have an idea of your own childhood traits but invariably there may be a few traits you 'grew out of' with age – and only those who raised you will be able to remember them.

My Childhood Traits

The best way I can convey the differences which can occur in traits between autistic children and autistic adults as well as how certain traits can develop with age, is to provide some background as to some of my own childhood traits.

AM I AUTISTIC?

Lack Of Self-Awareness/Hyposensitivity

Lack of self-awareness is well-documented in some (but not all) adult autistics, and particularly in autistic children where it can come across as if they are enclosed in a 'cocoon' or a 'world of their own'.

As a child I had this to the extreme – whilst I was always 'functional' and social I had almost zero self-awareness whatsoever and can say with hindsight I was pleasantly wrapped up in an invisible cocoon which protected me from the rather harsh realities of the outside world.

As a child I was also extremely hyperactive and hyposensitive (under-sensitive) to pain.

The specifics of this memory are quite vague but I do recall that around the age of 7 I somehow broke my leg on a slide and didn't even realise as I didn't feel any pain. I just noticed I landed very heavily and that the adults looked horrified and were rushing towards me. What bothered me the most was the itchiness caused by the plaster cast I had to wear for what felt like months afterwards (I loved the crutches though – I had great fun with them).

I also broke my arm at some point but I can't remember how; maybe I broke my arm on the slide and my leg somewhere else – I'm honestly not sure which way round it was because I had no self-awareness that I had broken something at the time – I just know I broke one or the other on that slide!

What I do remember very clearly is when, aged 8 I had just started climbing down from the top of a *huge* tree when the boys at the top of the tree thought it would be 'fun' to loosen the rope I was using to climb down; thereby plunging me *back first* the equivalent of two storeys to the ground. It later transpired I had crushed three vertebrate (two in my back, one in my neck) and narrowly avoided serious disability.

AM I AUTISTIC?

I still remember *that* accident with crystal clarity.

Once I realised what the boys were doing I had an 'instant preview' of what was going to happen next and knew I was going *down*. I quickly threw off the *'Thundercats'* sword I had strapped to my back before instantly plunging to the ground.

Once on the ground, obviously I couldn't move and the stupid boys were of course stuck up the tree, as they hadn't given any thought as to how they might now get down themselves.

Luckily, fairly quickly the very tall (must have been well over 6ft) much older brother of one of the boys came running out from the house. I remember he looked like he was in a state of panic and kept asking me if I was ok.

I wasn't in any pain, and everything was still (I am assuming I was in a state of shock). I kept trying to say *'they undid the rope'*, but all that came out was garbage.

When I could hear myself speaking in what sounded like computer babble I started getting panicked and confused that the words I was hearing in my head were not coming out of my mouth the same way.

The brother then picked me up (not technically the best thing to do in this scenario – it would have been best to call an ambulance who would have put me on a stretcher to avoid any further damage; but he was only about 19), and someone drove me to the doctors who of course put me straight in an ambulance.

I can't remember anything after that.

I still don't know how I found the speed, clarity or dexterity to hold myself on the rope with one hand whilst untying and hurling away the sword with the other all in a matter of seconds, what I do know is as soon as they loosened the rope I instantly saw a 'moving image' of me on the floor with the (bulky, plastic) sword breaking my back in two.

Whilst I didn't have any 'fear' at that point (there was no time for fear), the image showed me that if I didn't lose the sword whatever fate awaited me when I greeted the ground was going to be *extremely* unpleasant.

In hindsight I would say this is my 'autistic visual thinking' at its best; that picture of me on the ground spoke to me quicker than my thoughts could have done and gave me a chance to respond in a situation where there wasn't time to 'think' about what was happening.

In the months afterwards I wasn't happy about being made to take a term off school and being confined to a wheelchair with a neck brace for several months to recover as I didn't feel any pain. To me it felt physically as if nothing had happened so often I would just mess around and then quickly get in the wheelchair whenever someone was in the vicinity!

Don't Go Near The Water...

When I was around 9 or 10 I had a bad accident at a fishing lake. I was there with the man who raised me and he was fishing at the top of the bank whilst I was edging closer to the water to try and improve my chances.

Unfortunately, it was a very steep, wet, muddy bank and I soon went sliding at great speed all the way down the bank towards the water. As I went in feet first I went all the way under, deep into the water. As it was a trout lake there were lots of rushes and underwater vegetation which I got tangled up in and I was there for what seemed like a while before the man who raised me inched his own way down the bank and hauled me out.

Thanks to my 'cocoon' the whole experience felt rather calm – I had no sensation of the water or the cold, I was just aware it was very dark,

I was very deep under the water, I had no sense of weight and seemed to be held in 'suspense' for some reason.

When I was eventually hauled out I wanted to continue fishing and was very disappointed when we had to drive back to the hotel.

The water experiences didn't end there unfortunately.

When I was 10/11 years old I dived into the shallow end of a swimming pool (mistaking it for the deep end) smashing the bottom half of my front teeth to smithereens.

At around 14/15 I went on a geography field trip and at this point I have to say my memory is failing me because I can't remember whether a classmate on the trip fell into the water and I laughed so hard I fell in as well, or if it was the other way round.

All I remember is; *we both ended up in the water.*

I thought this was *hilarious* - she didn't - and we ended up having a grand display of fisticuffs and attempts at mutual drowning in the water (!).

To contrast these traits with me as an *adult,* I have come full-circle and now you won't catch me getting in a swimming pool because it's always cold and I don't like the way the water burns my nose and bothers me for hours afterwards; as an adult I've developed fairly normal 'sensitivities' where previously I was *hypo*sensitive (although I think my younger self might say I've just 'gone soft').

Lack Of Body Awareness (Proprioception)

If a clinician was to ask the woman who raised me about my childhood traits; aside from the hyperactivity she would say that I was incredibly clumsy (and that would be true).

I grew up in a large house with a woman who was particularly fond of her expensive china/glass ornaments which were dotted around every shelf and table in every single room and hallway of the house.

She would *not be happy* when I would be rushing around and knock over some of her favourite bone china.

And this would happen *a lot.*

As an adult I am aware of my natural clumsiness and have spent years correcting it as best I can. So these days, it would be unlikely to be the first thing someone says about me because I've successfully *minimised* this trait.

School Years

During my high school years I went to a Convent school.

It started off well.

I got 96% in the English exam at the end of my first year, rapidly propelling me to the top of the year group for English out of 120+ pupils (I still remember the mark because no-one was more surprised than me).

As an Ambassador for *Potential Plus UK*, a UK charity which works to provide a more supportive learning experience for high potential/ gifted children, I should probably say it would have been great if the school had a programme which recognised which children had 'high potential' and then enrolled me on some sort of mentoring scheme to help make sure I achieved it; certainly in my case as I worked through my school years it would have been useful if my teachers had assumed I was 'smart' instead of just viewing me as 'trouble'.

Then they might have stopped getting frustrated every time I would question their 'facts' that were either not true (seemed to stem from the teacher's subjective view of things) or seemed to be lacking in hard evidence to support them.

AM I AUTISTIC?

In any case, there was no mentoring programme.

Instead, for my 'reward' I got compulsorily-enrolled into Latin class; which is where they enlisted everyone who got a high grade in English.

And I *hated* Latin.

I saw no point in spending two years learning a 'dead' language; I wanted *out.*

The school wouldn't let me transfer into another class, so instead I got very bored and restless.

One day I passed around a 'scratch and sniff' picture of a nude fireman because I thought it was a much more amusing alternative to snotty Latin.

A few girls in the class scratched a bit off and passed it to the next person – the idea being to eventually reveal the 'hose' (some also gave it a sniff which I thought was extra-hilarious – ugh!).

Then the Latin teacher saw it and my wish was granted; there was no more Latin for me.

I was promptly removed from Latin and transferred to German instead (which I also hated but at least there were 'German Picnics' twice a year where we got to spend the whole lesson sampling the different foods and doing no work – they were a winner).

I have read in some articles related to what was formerly known as Asperger's that they often list *'Oppositional'* as a trait. Oppositional as in challenging the views of an 'authority' figure and defiantly refusing to do as asked if requested instructions are not agreed with.

I have an issue with the above description; I think it should be modified to *'extremely unlikely to do anything without a credible and justifiable reason for doing so – and definitely unlikely to do anything just because someone with a fancy title asked them to'.*

Maybe I'm being oppositional.

I had multiple suspensions, detentions and even an expulsion (later reversed) at the Convent and when I was doing a whole term of 'lunch time detention' the Deputy Head (who was indeed a Nun) kept insisting I ate my lunch *standing up* in the corner of the lunch hall, facing the wall near the entrance (so everyone could see).

Apparently, scrubbing the tables for a whole term was not enough – an extra dose of humiliation was required as well.

Anyway, this did not happen.

Not once.

Every lunch time my dear friend who was on lunchtime detention with me dutifully ate her sandwiches standing up in the corner, facing the wall.

Every lunch time the Nun would follow me round furiously shouting at me to get me to do the same.

Every lunch time I would completely ignore her, get my lunch and eat it *sitting at a table.*

I had decided that I was going to get on with the lunchtime detentions (I scrubbed more tables and crushed more cans than a professional) as I wanted to pass my exams and have a career; which wouldn't have happened if I'd been expelled.

However, standing up facing the wall to eat lunch was just 'not appropriate'.

It was draconian and designed for no reason other than to humiliate us, it was *unreasonable*; therefore I was just not going to do it.

And I never did, not once.

In the end she gave up, stopped following me round ranting and instead would stand by the door and glare at me.

So then I just made sure to sit with my back to her and that was the end of that.

Attention Deficit Hyperactivity 'Disorder' (ADHD)

Yes I am ADHD (self-diagnosed).

Is it a 'disorder' for me? No.

Whilst this trait is not an autistic trait it is quite common in some (but not all) autistic children and adults.

According to the DSM-5 (Diagnostic and Statistical Manual of Mental Disorders), one of the diagnostic criteria for this 'disorder' is that the person seems to *'Become bored with a task after only a few minutes, unless doing something enjoyable'*.

This last part is important as one thing people don't often realise about ADHD is that it is a double-edged sword; those with no interest in something (like Latin class), will get unbearably fidgety and bored. However, when 'something of interest' does capture the attention of an ADHD person they will often be the most intensely focused person in the room.

I used to know someone who had a 'statemented' (i.e. officially diagnosed) ADHD child and he had no interest in academic subjects in class yet would become hyper-focused when playing video games or at his karate class.

When playing video games he became *so* focused he wouldn't let anything detract from his attention to the point where he wouldn't even break for the toilet; so he would wet himself instead – without interrupting his playing.

That's rather extreme but I think that appropriately represents the double-edged sword of ADHD.

If an ADHD person channels that 'hyper-focus' in the right direction (which I try and do with my work), they can work at hyper-speed with extreme levels of concentration.

In my case, a good example of how my ADHD materialised at school would be in my A-Level Business Studies class.

At the start of the year, the teacher had under-estimated me (as they usually did) and after splitting up me and my 'share-a-joke' partner in crime to opposite ends of the classroom, regularly proceeded to take up residence on my desk resting her (rather large and not in any way pleasant to look at) behind on the table with her back to me whilst she then addressed the rest of the class.

As her teaching style was very lazy (primarily spending 20 minutes reading a section from the textbook which I'd already read through in about 10 seconds as soon as we were on the page), I taught myself at home and got bored in the lesson itself.

This style of teaching combined with my not wanting to look at her 'behind' for the whole lesson, led to me going off 'wandering' round the rest of the school for about 20 minutes at a time.

Each lesson.

I had these types of 'unspoken agreements' with some teachers.

My French teacher let me complete my English homework in her lessons as I clearly wasn't interested in French (which ironically I'm now learning via an App on my phone – it is a beautiful language).

The Business Studies teacher ignored my wandering and we all got on.

When it was results time for the first half of the A-Level I went with my friends to get my results and we were all (even me for once) left completely speechless when the woman who had sat with her back to me for the last year suddenly greeted me with open arms; *'Here's my Star!!!'* she said before flinging her arms round me and waving a bit of paper (I tried not to gag – it was a personal space invasion of the highest order).

It transpired I got an 'A'.

After that she sat at her own desk for the rest of the year.

I still went wandering.

Although *Wikipedia* sometimes has issues with 'subjective editing', it is generally quite useful as a starting point to find out more information on a topic. As such I am including a segment from their record on ADHD which I found quite interesting (full link can be found in the *References & Further Reading* section at the end of this guide).

As ADHD is common, natural selection likely favored the traits, at least individually, and they may have provided a survival advantage. For example, some women may be more attracted to males who are risk takers, increasing the frequency of genes that predispose to ADHD in the gene pool. As it is more common in children of anxious or stressed mothers, some argue that ADHD is an adaptation that helps children face a stressful or dangerous environment with, for example, increased impulsivity and exploratory behavior.

Hyperactivity might have been beneficial, from an evolutionary perspective…in certain environments it may have offered advantages to the individuals themselves, such as quicker response to predators or superior hunting skills.

I support the above view and note that under 'societal causes' the following entry is listed:

'Behavior typical of ADHD occur more commonly in children who have experienced violence and emotional abuse'.

Whilst I'm sure most ADHD children have *not experienced abuse,* I can vouch from my own experience that growing up in an abusive household greatly exacerbates ADHD traits in children.

To show how this trait can change from childhood to adulthood I would like to highlight that once I finally ceased all contact with the people who raised me, my stress levels and ADHD traits have reduced by about 70%.

The remaining 30% I put into my work and I am quite disciplined about following a daily 'detox routine' with lots of water, fresh air/ exercise and healthy eating (artificial additives do make me hyper!) to ensure I get the benefits of this trait – via my work – without the downsides and that my life remains as calm and stress-free as possible.

About 15 minutes' walk from my house there is a forested area with a boating lake which I find very relaxing to walk round and sit by when I have lots of energy and start getting a bit 'restless'. I find being by water and areas of natural beauty really helps relax me when I'm working long hours.

Overall, this trait has been of great benefit to my work coaching clients and also in social settings *with people I'm comfortable with,* as I have extremely high levels of personal motivation and find it easy to motivate other people and have a good time; my brain is naturally wired for 'up'.

Whilst I can be quite stringent about my own personal routines, I do find I am much more flexible around children and having lots of energy is useful for entertaining my nieces when they stay over for a weekend.

I do notice 'hyperactive traits' in those parents who have the most fun with their children when they are out and about and this is why I would challenge the clinical view of ADHD as always being a 'Disorder' and the preference in the US for using prescription drugs on children with this trait.

Taste Sensitivities

As a child I had major taste sensitivities.

When I was younger, dinner times at home would always be an ordeal as I would get terribly distressed if egg yolk spilled over and touched a chip as the chip was then 'contaminated' (it also later transpired I am allergic to egg yolk).

I also wouldn't touch animal innards such as 'liver' which unfortunately seemed to be a favourite dish in a household where any 'disobedience' resulted in being made to 'sit at the table' until everything was gone or being sent to the dreaded 'naughty step' – or worse.

Although none of this would work as I *just wouldn't touch it.*

So I would often be sat at the table on my own for some length of time.

Conversely, lunchtimes at primary school were fine because I could leave any 'contaminated' items on the plate without fear of reprisal.

As a child I only really liked one sandwich; 'ham, cheese and pickle'. I would eat just ham, just beef or just chicken sandwiches if I *had to* but I really didn't like it if they had been 'contaminated' with any other fillings; for example I really didn't like the taste of butter and meat slices together.

Essentially I just liked ham, cheese and pickle (no butter).

I also had major issues with the taste and consistency of liquids; I didn't like the taste of water or squash and therefore wouldn't touch a drop.

As a result I had at least three trips to the ER as a child due to the resulting dehydration and er…difficulties going to the loo.

As going to the ER wasn't a pleasant experience (I'll spare you the details), the final time I went I resolved to never have to go there again and started to force myself to drink squash. I also acquired a taste for apple juice and would drink that by the gallon.

As an adult I now drink two litres of water a day and have done for years which shows how I've *grown out of* this taste sensitivity with age.

Stimming

When I was a younger child in a cot (maybe 2-3 years old - not sure exactly) I started obsessively sucking my thumb and scratching/ rubbing my face at the same time.

Excessive rubbing of the face is a common 'stim' in some autistic children and I had to wear mittens up until about 5 years old to prevent me scratching my cheeks to pieces.

My sister has since advised me (and I have confirmed this with them directly) that the people who raised me had a policy of never getting up in the night to check in on me when I was crying as a baby; I was adopted at 6 months old and spent my first four months with my birth mother in a hostel for homeless mothers, followed by two months with foster parents before I was placed with my adoptive parents so I would assume I was probably a bit unsettled – hence the crying.

Apparently I would cry all night until I fell asleep from exhaustion and this continued every night for months which was very distressing for my then 13 year old sister as she was forbidden from checking up on me.

One of my earliest memories is being 'cuffed' in my cot with these wretched mittens every night and waking up to find that I was still cuffed for what felt like hours every morning when all I wanted to do was rub my face (which I found soothing), but I couldn't so I was very, very, very stressed.

Whilst I grew out of this 'stim' with age, on reflection I think it was triggered by the stress of growing up in an environment where I had a difficult upbringing by the people who raised me.

I got that phrase from my sister after she explained why it is not appropriate to call them 'parents'; although they raised us in a luxurious house in a very affluent area and they were always careful to put on a good 'show' to the outside world with lavish birthday parties etc., they were seriously neglectful inside the house and beyond the superficial did not fulfil the role of 'parent' in a conventional sense.

I considered this view for a couple of years and after combining my personal experiences with how I saw my sister treated and reading the observations social workers made on my family situation after I requested a copy of my social service records (I was placed in foster care several times from the age of 5), I now agree it is a more appropriate phrase.

As an adult I rarely stand still. I often 'bounce' or 'sway' slightly from side to side when preparing food or waiting for something to cook. I don't do it because I'm stressed, I just find it soothing – I never even recognised it as an autistic 'stim' until I started writing this guide. I'm not sure that it would be terribly noticeable as it is quite subtle; but I wouldn't do it in public.

I have included the above information to illustrate how stims are often very soothing for autistic children and adults. Most stims are not self-injurious like mine was in childhood, but some are.

Special Interests

When I was around 6 I got an Atari XE and taught myself how to programme on it. Programming code wasn't enjoyable for me (it took a lot of work to render one uninspiring line on the monitor) and the games were frankly - a bit rubbish.

Around the age of 7 I got a Nintendo Entertainment System (NES) and LOVED IT.

I started playing games and reading video games magazines obsessively; video games were my first 'special interest'.

I expanded on this interest (aged around 8 or 9) by deciding to publish my own video games magazine and I strategically planned all the different sections; news, previews, reviews and the different scoring metrics (graphics, sound, difficulty levels etc.) and assessed what games to include. I then played the games to death, sat at the typewriter (!) and painstakingly typed up my magazine before hand-drawing the cover image (drawing is not my strong point) and selling a few copies to my friends for 10p each.

I had the foresight to call them 'limited editions' because I would only ever type up two or three copies of each.

This is quite a specific trait to have as a child.

As a teenager, the highlight of my week was tuning in to the Official Charts every Sunday as I found the movements of certain songs up and down the charts fascinating. Every Monday I would always insist that after school on the walk to the bus stop my friends stopped off at 'Our Price' the local record store, so that I could see the extended chart positions for songs that weren't covered on the Radio Top 40. I would also easily be able to recite the entry or highest chart positions of certain 'tracks of interest' a year later if my friends mentioned the song or the artist, although I quickly stopped doing this – the girls from my school *were not interested* in these facts…!

Everything Changes, Everything Stays The Same

I've realised just recently that I've come full circle from my 8 year old self and ended up running a growing publishing venture; first it published *The New Idealist* magazine *(currently on hiatus but still available online with 15,000+ downloads/online reads to date and growing at time of writing)*, then *ShortStorySunday.com* (a site for those who love short stories), and now I'm publishing this guide which is picking up from where *The Autism Issue* of *The New Idealist* left off.

So whilst my 'special interests' have changed, the 'publishing' trait itself has remained unchanged into adulthood.

In Summary

These (and other) childhood traits are the sort of thing the clinicians will take into account when assessing whether someone is autistic or whether they simply happen to share some autistic traits.

If you aren't keen on going for a formal diagnosis and prefer the route to self-diagnosis, you should find that your childhood traits will be the last piece of the puzzle.

Chapter 7

AUTISM: THE SELF-DIAGNOSIS PROCESS

How To Self-Diagnose

By the time you have reached this part of the guide the previous chapters should have provided you with a fairly clear idea of whether or not you are autistic or whether you simply happen to share some autistic traits.

For those of you who feel fairly certain that you are indeed autistic – welcome to the club!

At this point you might want to consider putting this guide down for a week or two to digest this news as the next steps in this process can be quite exhausting and it's probably already been a bit of a rollercoaster to reach this point.

Self-Diagnosis Or Formal Diagnosis?

The next step of this process is to decide whether you are happy with self-diagnosis alone or whether you think you would benefit from a formal diagnosis from a medical clinician.

Pros & Cons Of Self-Diagnosis

Pros

- You can do it yourself!

- You will not be officially diagnosed with having a 'mental disorder' or disability.

• You can remain outside of the clinical system and do not need to go through the lengthy and often draining process that a formal diagnosis requires.

• You will not need to involve your parents or siblings in your diagnosis (their views are often required as part of the formal diagnosis process).

• You can choose what being autistic means to you as you won't be legally subject to the 'autism is an impairment and disorder' driven views of the clinical system.

• No one else will know your autistic status unless you want them to.

Cons

• If you are not officially diagnosed you may have difficulty accessing autism support groups.

• You might find that other people question the validity of your diagnosis.

• If you have very disabling sensory difficulties that prevent you from finding work you will not be able to claim government benefits without a formal diagnosis.

• If you disclose your autistic status to your friends/family or colleagues you may still encounter the same discrimination and stigma that affects those who are clinically diagnosed.

The Journey Of A Self-Diagnosed Autistic

I realised I was autistic one month after I turned 32.

At time of writing that is exactly two years ago.

It seems like a short time in calendar years yet a lifetime in my years as I've always known since my earliest years that I was fundamentally 'different' to my peers; autism is now the convenient 'label' that explains why.

When I watched the HBO film *'Temple Grandin'* on TV over the festive break two years ago I was expecting to watch something quite interesting.

I wasn't expecting to be searching 'autism traits' on my phone before the credits rolled in a full-on state of panic that a lot of the 'unusual' traits that I have – that I thought were unique to me – Temple seemed to have too; and those traits were what made her *autistic*.

My gut knew before I'd even booted up the search page; it was true, I was *autistic*.

But hang on.

Before I'd had a chance to digest this 'news' the page loaded and I found myself on the website of the *National Autistic Society (NAS)*. My head started spinning when I was confronted with the apparent *'Triad of Impairments'* that autistic people have. The web page was a long list of negativity – autism meant; 'a lifelong disability', 'spectrum disorder', 'difficulty with social communication', 'difficulty with social interaction', 'difficulty with social imagination' and on and on and on. The pages of negative descriptions left me so confused; my gut (which is always right) was loudly telling me when I saw *Temple Grandin* that I had finally found 'it'; what makes me different to everyone else, yet my head was spinning because I knew I was more than a *'Triad of Impairments'*.

Yes, I knew I found it difficult to connect to most (but not all) people beyond a superficial level and had specific traits which have hindered me in the workplace and at social events. I knew I met at least one of each of the *'Triad of Impairments'* (although I would consider them to be 'differences' rather than 'impairments'), but I also knew I had traits which were clearly beneficial and I did not have a *'disorder'* or a *'serious, lifelong and disabling condition'*.

After flicking through a few pages I had enough, I decided I couldn't possibly be autistic based on that description and closed the browser; before proceeding to have a full on sensory overload at the conflicting messages of everything I had just seen and read.

And so started my self-diagnosis journey.

It was several months before I could bring myself to look into autism again (although I thought about it every day), and the next time I looked I pointedly avoided the NAS site and found myself on the *'Wrong Planet'* forum. From there I found out there were tests I could do and promptly completed the AQ Test scoring 32 (well within the 'you are likely to be autistic' range) and the Aspie Quiz (Final Version 2) – generating an Aspie score of 141/200 and a neurotypical (non-autistic) score of 92/200 along with a shiny graph and a rating of *'You are very likely an Aspie'*.

By this point the tests were loudly telling me I had strong autistic traits but I was extremely reluctant to accept this as the ghost of *'The Triad of Impairments'* hovered over my head.

I was now obsessed (and I mean *obsessed*) with finding out everything there was to know about autism – mainly I was looking for something positive because I didn't want to label myself with anything negative.

I looked and looked but there just didn't seem to be anything *positive* written about being autistic; my positive traits had no home.

Was it possible that as I had *positive* autistic traits I couldn't be autistic? That didn't make any sense.

Maybe it was time to go for a formal diagnosis?

I am rarely nervous but I found myself getting some fairly unpleasant butterflies when I called up the 'dreaded' NAS to ask for some information on getting a diagnosis. To their credit I got through straightaway and the lady on the phone was very helpful and emailed me some material on the formal diagnosis process very quickly.

The guide started off well; *'A lot of people say their diagnosis has helped them to understand why they have difficulties with some things and why they are especially good at some things'*

After reading this more balanced phrasing I found myself starting to think *'OK, this could be an option'*.

Yet as I read on my gut started churning as the difficulty of getting a formal diagnosis was explained. The guide advised that you have to present a strong case as to why being autistic is a difficulty to your GP to get them to refer you; and this should involve highlighting one trait from each of the dreaded *'Triad of Impairments'*.

I had another read and accepted that whilst a lot of the 'impairments' didn't apply to me, my sensory sensitivities and some of the traits that I had such as my preference for in-depth conversations and difficulty processing the 'social banter' which a lot of people – particularly men – seem to use in place of 'proper' conversation were making it more difficult for me to integrate in social settings as I got older (which is why I thought it might be useful to talk to someone about them – although I now realise this type of practical support is extremely thin on the ground).

I was encouraged to see this note; *'It's important to add that many people with autism are imaginative (for example, they are accomplished writers, artists and musicians). If you're quite creative, this shouldn't automatically be taken as a sign that you do not have autism.'*

Whilst I knew instinctively that I did not *'have'* autism, I *'was'* autistic, I was on board with the general sentiment.

I wasn't sure why the guide had a more 'balanced' tone than the website, but I trusted the information in the guide more than the information on the website.

This is why when I read the bit which said that *'adults with autism have been misdiagnosed with mental health problems such as schizophrenia'*, I knew immediately my road to 'formal diagnosis' had just reached an abrupt end.

And that was before I got to the bit that explained that once you have a diagnosis of autism you are legally classed as having a disability.

No way was I volunteering myself to be a) diagnosed with a 'lifelong' disability or b) mis-diagnosed with schizophrenia; and this was before I was aware that autism is officially classed a 'Mental Disorder' under the Mental Health Act – for some reason the guide doesn't explicitly state this.

I was aware by this point that there are people for whom being autistic is a severe disability (particularly if they have extreme sensory sensitivities which make it difficult to take a trip into town for work or food shopping for example), and that I had definite traits which held me back in many areas; but I knew that my autistic traits also propelled me forward in other areas and for me personally, this language all seemed incredibly negative and a bit extreme.

Everything was black and white; *'you are autistic and you have a long list of impairments and a disability'* (and apparently a *'mental disorder'* I later found out) – or you are not. If you were really unlucky you might hit the 'grey area' and find yourself mis-diagnosed as schizophrenic.

None of these options were winning me over.

After watching *Temple Grandin*, completing the tests and doing my research, by this point I had already (reluctantly) accepted I was autistic. I say reluctantly because nearly everything I had read online about autism was so clinical and so negative; it was frankly quite depressing to read.

Everything lacked 'colour' and this is what I felt being autistic meant to me (because like Temple Grandin – I am a visual thinker). *My picture* of autism constantly moved around and never stayed still because it was full of *life*.

In contrast, when I looked at the *clinical* definitions of autism I just saw a long line or narrow road cloaked in a *cold*, silent, grey mist which stretched as far as the eye could see. It was completely eerie and the absolute definition of 'soulless'.

Two years later; my view hasn't changed.

Hopefully this guide will help add some 'colour' into what is written about the autism spectrum.

My Autistic Traits

For those of you wondering how my traits led me to realise I am autistic; in addition to the childhood traits outlined in the previous chapter, I have summarised some of my key traits below.

Visual Sensitivities

I am a visual thinker and as such I can find certain ultra-realistic graphic depictions of gore or violence distressing. Recently, I was watching TV series *'The Leftovers'* and really enjoying it until the third or fourth episode had a truly horrendous 'stoning' scene which triggered off my sensitivities and ruined my whole evening.

I subsequently had to delete the other episodes as I thought if it was going to be 'that kind of show' I can't watch as I can't run the risk of seeing anything that graphic in that show again.

This was very irritating because I really liked the show up to that point, but alas; that was the end of that.

The positive aspect of this trait is that when problem solving I will tend to 'see' the answer to a problem rather than 'think' it. When I was in the penultimate year of primary school the teacher drew a really complex math problem on the board explaining that we wouldn't know how to answer it yet, but he would teach us how to solve it.

I had absolutely zero interest in maths but yet when the teacher was talking, something to do with the way he had visually arranged the problem on the board allowed me to 'see' the answer so I shouted it out – and was right.

The teacher was stunned and asked me to explain how I arrived at the answer – but I couldn't because I didn't process the problem in any logical maths-type way. I was at a loss myself to explain it and knew it was best not to talk about 'seeing the numbers move around on the board' because everyone would think I was (even more) odd, so I just shrugged my shoulders and for that one day I was the cool kid in class.

As an adult, when thinking about front covers for *The New Idealist* I would always 'see' the cover fully designed in my mind and then relay that idea to the designer to bring into reality. As I was always quite precise about describing the cover I saw, the designers usually did a very good job of replicating exactly what I saw – even though I can't design for toffee.

On the flip-side, I suspect some of the designers thought I was a 'quite difficult' to work with because I would hire them to deliver my cover concept rather than create their own.

Noise Sensitivities

I am hypersensitive to certain frequencies of noise.

I can get quite unsettled by the noise of a car revving in the street whilst idle and quite distressed by the sound of a motorbike. It's not the 'loudness' of the noise, it's the frequency - it's like it travels right through my *gut* and makes it vibrate at the deepest level in a really unpleasant way.

Emergency sirens are equally distressing but as they are on a different frequency they have no effect on my body and seem to vibrate around my *brain* instead.

After I've heard a siren, although it won't display on the outside I am inwardly quite distressed and distracted for about 5-10 minutes afterwards. Whilst I get over it quite quickly, I am aware in some autistics this distress can last several hours at a time which is when it starts to tip into 'autism can be a disability' territory.

When watching TV I always have to sit with a control in hand to mute the adverts as they always seem to come on a bit louder than the TV show and that noisy pitch and frequency really rattles round my head.

Similarly, whilst I seem immune to a certain 'pitch' of raised voice – however loud it gets, there is a certain pitch of shouting I can't stand (although that might be more due to my family background) and as a result I can't have 'shouty soaps' like *Eastender*s on the TV; not even in the background because all the noise and rowing makes my brain start to overload.

Conversely, I LOVE music. I listen to it whilst working for several hours a day and often listen to it again on high quality headphones late at night before I go to bed. I particularly like dance music when I'm working as I have noticed the speed of the music matches the speed of my brain which is helps me work extremely quickly.

In contrast, I get distracted by 'little sounds'.

I have to turn my watch over and place it at the far end of the bedside table when I sleep and when I stay at my sister's I have to remove the batteries from the clock in the room to avoid the tiny but infuriating 'tick-tock' sound.

When I completed a music technology course a few years ago the class had to do a well-known test (the name of which I can't remember) where a certain frequency of 'noise' is played before it gets slowly turned down to zero. It is meant to show how sound has different frequencies and not everyone can hear each frequency. Apparently the older you get the less you hear.

The longer the noise played the more people would drop out as they couldn't hear it anymore, by the end it was just me (age 30) and an 18 year old left and I think this demonstrates how autistic people with noise sensitivities can hear sounds at frequencies people without sensitivities can't and why we can get incredibly agitated at what seems like 'nothing' to someone else.

Whilst I can't read sheet music I can play musical instruments (particularly the piano), by ear quite well and did get through to the semi-final stage of a large international songwriting contest a few times.

Unfortunately, I had to stop writing and playing music a couple of years ago after I decided not to pursue a career in the music industry; my 'obsessive' trait means that I can't just 'casually' write or play music without getting completely consumed by it.

As a result I won't go near the keyboard as I can't do anything by 'halves' – it's all or nothing.

I do miss writing music though.

Repetitive Behaviour/Routines/Details

I like lining up objects.

Like a few other 'quirks' I have, I didn't recognise this as an *autistic* trait until I thought I might be autistic and started researching the traits in more detail.

At the weekend, when I sit down for breakfast in front of the TV, I have to line up my liquid vitamin supplement, smoothie, water glass, water bottle and carrot sticks by height order or I can't relax because it's all too disorganised.

Even when I'm watching a programme with no adverts, I can't put the TV remote on the table because its bulky size just doesn't 'fit' with the other objects and looks unsightly.

So I put it by my lap instead; out of the view of my eyeline.

One of my cats has now realised that one of the best ways to get my attention is to sit on the table when I'm watching TV and hover *dangerously close* to my neatly lined up objects whilst staring at me. Shooing her away doesn't work so I am then forced to invite her onto my lap simply to get her out of my eyeline and reduce the risk of her flicking tail distributing cat dander into my pristine glass of water…

When I stay in a hotel I have to *immediately* clear away all of the leaflets and cardboard signs they have littering the tables into a drawer because I can't stand the clutter; it's just too disorganised.

I can drive my romantic partners a bit crazy because I request to change room in 50% of the hotel rooms I check into if the room or the view isn't perfectly symmetrical.

I just can't relax in a wonky room or a room with a 'blighted' view.

Same applies to restaurant tables.

I can't sit at a table in the middle of a busy thoroughfare because I can't have waiters or diners bustling around my personal space so will frequently request to change to a quieter area.

Same applies to drinks.

When I was younger my favourite sandwich was a 'ham, cheese and pickle' sandwich. I would happily eat that sandwich every day but would get very upset if it was just a ham and cheese or just a ham and pickle sandwich; I wouldn't like it at all.

As an adult my favourite alcoholic drink is a 'rum and coke' and like the ham, cheese and pickle sandwich this relatively simple drink seems to cause me a huge amount of issues.

I can't just have a 'rum and coke'.

It has to be 'dark rum, full sugar coke, three quarters coke/one quarter rum' and *absolutely no ice.*

I can take or leave the slice of lime.

When ordering this drink myself I will make sure it's made as above. About 50% of the time the server will put ice in before tipping the drink away and making it again without ice (ice dilutes the flavour so I won't drink one with ice in).

The Joys Of Autistic Dating

On a date this drink will go back about 75% of the time as they rarely get it right.

These days I can generally tell within 5 minutes whether a date is going to go well based on whether or not they get that order right.

If they can remember those little details I will like them more because unfortunately there are lots of little 'details' that need taking care of for anyone who dates me and someone either gets them and just handles them with ease or they get agitated; and I'm not going to be interested in anyone who gets agitated.

So, if they put down a glass rammed with ice; chances of a second date are looking slim.

Often they put the drink down and then remember I said *no ice*, and go back and get another one.

With this one there's still hope.

In case you're wondering why on earth these women bother; because I get details - *I am extremely good at looking after someone else's 'details'.*

If someone I'm dating has any of their own quirks or quibbles I just go with the flow because I understand that taking care of details reduces stress and that means more time spent enjoying the evening.

As a result I do often end up dating other extremely fussy 'perfectionist' type women because they 'get' my details, I 'get' theirs and we generally have a very nice time.

I'm not sure if that's everyone's idea of romance but it works for me.

Social Faux Pas – I Don't Like Boy George

I am the person who points out the elephant in the room.

Often this is considered a 'social faux pas' however I usually tend to disagree and feel like I'm just stating the obvious; it's not really my problem if other people don't like it – it doesn't make it any less true.

An example would be my interest with how British musician Boy George – *a convicted criminal who received a 15 month prison sentence for the vicious assault and false imprisonment of a male escort* – is still lauded by major media networks like the BBC.

Boy George has featured on BBC Radio 2's 'Sounds of the 80s' twice since his release – he was one of the first guests to feature on the new show in 2012 before returning to the show in 2014 for a full length performance with the BBC Philharmonic Orchestra; the same year he was also invited to perform with his reformed band on BBC One prime time TV show 'Strictly Come Dancing'.

As a result the victim now has to watch his suffering trivialised by the mass media who carry on giving the convicted criminal air time and interviews as if nothing happened.

I can't imagine that this would be the case if the victim was a woman so I wonder if the victim's life somehow has less value in the eyes of others because he is a man and they don't really understand the concept of male-on-male assault? Or is it because he was an escort? Or maybe it's written off as a 'gay thing'? If not any of these then what?

Seeing such systematic displays of a lack of empathy makes me bristle when I hear debates around autistic people showing an apparent 'lack of empathy'. I tend to think this would be a view espoused by the same type of person who watches that man on the TV or hears him on the radio and jigs along to his songs without a single thought for the crime he committed when he handcuffed someone he had previously 'paid for' to a wall against their will before viciously beating them; the victim only got free by wrenching the fixture he was chained to *off the wall* and running down the street nearly *naked* in a state of terror.

This might be pointing out the 'elephant in the room' but some of us autistics can be good at that can't we?

(An interesting news article on this story can be found in the References & Further Reading section at the end of this guide).

Systemising

Whilst researching this guide I completed the SQ-R test and scored 90 – this is very high. In fact it's nearly 13 points higher than most autistics who take the test (who average 77.2 according to the 2005

SQ-R study) and nearly 35 points higher than the average non-autistic person (who average 55.6 according to the same study).

Previously, I did the original SQ test (which had a different scoring key) and scored 45 compared to the average of 24 for women and 30 for men.

Below, I've also included a snapshot of my recent Aspie Quiz (Final Version 3) results which seem to match the results of the SQ-R test. In the Aspie Quiz I score 10/10 in the *'Intellectual'* part of the spectrum relating to *'Aspie Talent'* which measures traits such as *'figuring out how things work'*, *'noticing details'*, *'finding patterns'*, *'making connections between things'*, *'unusual imagination'*, *'solving problems in unusual ways'* and *'unique ideas'*.

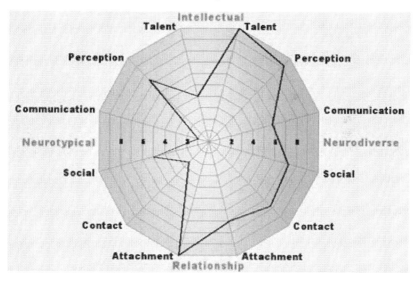

Broadly speaking, both test results are indicating I have an *'above average ability for analysing and exploring a system'*.

This I would agree with as I am aware that alongside my sensory sensitivities, systemising is my defining autistic trait; I am always analysing different systems.

Whatever task I may be doing, whenever I'm out for a walk or going to the cinema, my brain is *always* systemising (since I turned 30 it's been social and political systems, in my twenties it was music and business systems).

Deconstructing a system for me involves breaking it down into pieces, looking for the 'rules' behind the system and identifying every possible 'variable' which can affect a person's journey through the system (for better or worse).

In case you're wondering; I don't find the constant systemising stressful – it's what goes on in the 'world of my own' that I live in.

Once I've deconstructed a system and identified the rules and the variables I will have a good idea of what works and what doesn't. In other words, much like a mathematician analysing the odds at the casino, I will identify the ways in the which the system is 'loaded' against some participants and the ways in which it works for other participants; some workings are obvious, some less so and some are 'hidden' and rendered invisible to all but those with an eye for the tiniest of details.

Once I've identified the rules and variables I then look at how the system can be reconstructed in a fairer and more balanced way (fairness and balance are the rules that I'm driven by; they are hardwired into my DNA).

Although, obviously, this is not as easy as it sounds.

Whoever creates the system invents the rules and much like a person who consistently 'beats the house' at a casino, anyone who finds a way to get the rules working for them in ways the creator of the system didn't intend, will often find themselves excluded from the system completely.

Here are some examples of my systemising:

The Careers System – The Original System

When I set up my career management agency age 23 in 2004 I found a niche. The process of applying for jobs ran to specific rules and I had found a formula which worked which I could offer to other people to benefit from to help them get interviews and promotions.

2,000+ clients and tons of testimonials later; I think I've done a good job.

The Business System – No Place For Ethics

In my early twenties I launched lots of little business ideas; some worked some didn't. My overall view was that it is near-impossible to make money *ethically* within the UK business system – and I don't want to be involved in anything that isn't fair and balanced.

To further compound this point I have recently had to take a major reduction in turnover to my main business (the career management agency), since I found out *Google* – who I spend 90% of my advertising budget with – are partnering with the controversial organisation *Autism Speaks* on the '*Ten Thousands Genome Program (AUT10K)*' project to help find a possible cure for autism.

As part of this project, *Google* are providing the vast cloud-based database that the researchers will use to share genetic information on 'autistic patients'.

I worked out I've paid around £20,000 in the last 10 years' to *Google* in search advertising fees and am deeply unhappy at the thought of even just one more penny going towards funding such deeply unethical research.

As a result I've had to switch off all *Google* advertising for the business and have predictably seen my income plunge as a result.

After 10 inspiring years I'm now having to take steps to wind down my career management agency and look for other ways to generate an income that don't involve marketing with *Google*.

After analysing and working in this system in various roles since I graduated, I've concluded this is a system where there *really is no place for ethics*.

The Music Industry System – More Corporate Than It Appears

In my late twenties I was big into songwriting, got nominated for a couple of awards and wanted to be an 'anonymous songwriter/ producer' who signed people to my own independent label and stayed behind the scenes writing music for other people.

This required a test release of my own EP so I could explore the process for everything – and it was really interesting. Ultimately commercial success in the music industry relies on radio play and in the UK there are just two big popular music networks who all <u>set their own rules</u> as to what gets played and these rules are surprisingly un-meritocratic.

Ultimately I decided that it's a very tightly run system with limited flexibility and rules that did not appeal; I decided that in order to preserve my love of music I needed to avoid the music industry.

The New Idealist – Social/Political Systems

The New Idealist magazine was a continuation of my interest in social/ political systems and was designed to help me explore the way the world works in my areas of interest.

It wasn't set up as a commercial venture and I had an 8 issue (2 year) timescale for it, which I budgeted would be enough until my money ran out and would have covered all my areas of interest.

Unfortunately it burnt through money quicker than anticipated and so I tried some ideas to see if the magazine could support itself – whilst remaining free of charge and not carrying third party advertising.

They all failed.

Simultaneously I was exploring creating a sort of political group behind it as originally *'The New Idealist'* was meant to be a group of politically like-minded people with the magazine originally devised as a newsletter with which the group would communicate with.

I initially shelved this plan after deciding the group idea had too many variables.

However once I launched the magazine I decided to return to the original idea.

So I did a little concept test following Issue 2 and found what I predicted originally; when dealing with a wide range of people and a variety of ideas – there are just too many variables and everything is a bit disorganised and unpredictable.

My key goal was to get the magazine read 10,000 times and open up new doors for me to explore in my areas of interest; at time of writing the six issues have been read over 15,000 times and the magazine has helped me build a strong network of likeminded people as well as taking me in several new directions since I put it on hiatus.

So I would conclude it has been both a *predictable* financial disaster and a *surprise* success.

This concludes the summary of some of my key traits.

Chapter 8

AUTISM: THE CLINICAL DIAGNOSIS PROCESS

This chapter outlines the pros and cons of the formal diagnosis process in the UK and the US for those interested in pursuing this route.

Autism: The Clinical Diagnosis Process (UK)

UK clinicians tend to refer to the *World Health Organisation International Classification of Diseases* (ICD-10) which has the following definition:

Asperger syndrome

A disorder of uncertain nosological validity, characterized by the same kind of qualitativeabnormalities of reciprocal social interaction that typify autism, together with a restricted,stereotyped repetitive repertoire of interests and activities. The disorder differs from autism primarily in that there is no general delay or retardation in language or cognitive development. Most individuals are of normal intelligence but it is common for them to be markedly clumsy.

NHS Clinical Diagnosis Pathway

Those interested in a formal diagnosis on the NHS can expect to have to go through the following procedure:

> • Request a referral to a psychiatrist or clinical psychologist with a specialism in diagnosing Autism/Asperger's from your GP. Ensure you have prepared and presented a 'case' as to why your

autistic traits are causing you difficulty and why you should be referred; GPs are generally extremely reluctant to refer an adult who seems 'functional' for a diagnosis.

• If the GP agrees to refer it is likely you will be referred to the waiting list of a diagnostic service within your local Clinical Commissioning Group area or equivalent.

• Your diagnosis appointment will most likely be with a psychiatrist or a clinical psychologist with the diagnostic procedure varying depending on your geographical location and the individual evaluation preferences of the clinician you have been referred to; some may insist you complete 'screening questionnaires' including the AQ & EQ before they will offer you an appointment, some will just offer you an appointment.

• The use of screening questionnaires such as the AQ (Autism Spectrum Quotient) & EQ (Empathy Quotient) can result in you being 'screened out' of the process and refused a diagnosis appointment if you do not meet the required 'score' on paper. The use of the EQ questionnaire in particular can result in adults who meet the 'AQ' criteria yet display 'normal' levels of empathy on the questionnaire being declined an appointment for diagnosis. This is a result of those who designed the questionnaire holding the questionable view that autistic people are expected to display 'below normal levels of empathy', therefore any autistic person showing 'normal' or 'above average' levels of empathy (as measured by the EQ) can find they are unable to gain a formal diagnosis. As it is not possible to measure an emotion such as empathy on paper, this highly controversial and much-challenged theory is why this guide does not endorse the EQ test as part of the self-diagnosis process to find out whether or not you may be autistic.

• There are several 'diagnostic tools' available for clinicians to use during the actual diagnostic appointment, however clinicians are not required to use a specific diagnostic tool. DISCO - The Diagnostic Interview for Social and Communication Disorders - was developed by Dr. Lorna Wing and Dr. Judith Gould (the researchers behind the 'Triad of Impairments' theory of autism), and is a common diagnostic tool which involves a series of questions about your developmental history from when you were a young child. A clinician using DISCO will often require that you attend the appointment with a parent or sibling so that they can provide information on your childhood traits.

• Once the diagnostic evaluation is complete the diagnosing clinician will generally write to you to inform you of your diagnosis. As the process can be quite subjective and diagnosis is dependent on the individual view of the clinician who has the ability to diagnose any 'psychological condition' – not just autism; sometimes people can be given a diagnosis they were not expecting. As few psychologists or psychiatrists are experts in diagnosing autism (and even the ones who claim to be can hold 'subjective' views of autism), it is not uncommon for autistic people to be mis-diagnosed with another 'condition' such as schizophrenia. This is most likely because the traits of *social withdrawal, communication impairment, poor eye contact and speaking your thoughts out loud* are common in both schizophrenia *and* autism (although of course each autistic person is different and will not share all of the above traits). If the diagnosing clinician is not a specialist in autistic traits they may be unable to differentiate between the two and this is how mis-diagnosis occurs.

The Pros & Cons Of Formal Diagnosis

Pros

> • A formal diagnosis makes it easier to access autism support groups and specialist support services (where available).

> • A formal diagnosis provides eligibility to apply for disability benefits.

> • A formal diagnosis makes it more difficult for people to challenge your autistic status.

> • Some people find it comforting to have a formal diagnosis.

Cons

> • If you have 'acquired' reasonable social skills as an adult or developed 'coping mechanisms' to survive in a non-autistic environment and as a result seem to 'present normally' (in the eyes of a clinician), it can be incredibly difficult to get a referral for a diagnosis from your GP.

Women particularly suffer from this issue as they tend to find it easier to pick up social skills that 'mask' their autistic traits and many GPs are not aware that autistic traits often present differently in women.

> • If you are clinically diagnosed as autistic that means you are classed as having both a 'mental disorder' *and* a 'disability'. This can be an issue if you ever come into contact with 'official bodies' or want to challenge the way you have been treated in a healthcare, education, legal or employment setting for example, as you may now find that your opinions are considered 'less valid' than they were before your diagnosis. Some 'officials' may even deem you as *'not to having the capacity to make decisions'* under the 'Mental Capacity Act' and may request an opinion from your 'specialist' and defer to their view before

providing the service you have requested or making a decision on a complaint.

• Although a formal diagnosis should make it easier to access specialist support services in theory; in practice contact with your diagnosing clinician often ends at the point of diagnosis. This is due to NHS funding restrictions resulting in many diagnostic clinics offering a 'diagnosis-only' service without any follow-up appointments or additional support. If a key reason for seeking a formal diagnosis is to receive support with understanding and managing your autistic traits, the lack of post-diagnosis follow-up support can be very distressing for a newly diagnosed autistic person. This is because you will often be notified about your diagnosis via a letter in the mail yet find yourself unable to discuss your diagnosis with the diagnosing clinician as you will most likely have been 'cut-off' from receiving any further support from them.

• Many adults with a formal diagnosis find that there aren't any specialist services available in their local area as most autism-specific support services are targeted at autistic children while adult support groups are typically funded by charities and therefore extremely thin on the ground. If the newly-diagnosed adult receives no post-diagnosis support from their clinician and finds there isn't a specific support group in their local area they can feel very isolated as they will not have anyone to speak to about their diagnosis.

• It is common for autistic adults to be told that whilst they have autistic traits they do not meet the criteria for a clinical diagnosis; primarily because they have 'adapted well' and therefore do not 'need' one. If you are not presenting as having 'obvious severe impairments' due to your autistic traits the clinician will be reluctant to diagnose you; the issue is that those with 'minor impairments' or 'sensory issues' which are not obvious in the context of a diagnostic interview yet still act as a barrier to finding work or building a social circle will be refused a diagnosis and then find it extremely difficult to access any further support.

• If a mis-diagnosis of schizophrenia is made it can be extremely difficult to get the diagnosis reversed and this diagnosis will permanently remain on your medical records.

• Some clinicians will refuse to diagnose an autistic person who does not bring a parent or sibling to the diagnostic appointment as they will be unable to assess your childhood traits. A full overview of your childhood traits is important for the reasons outlined in *Chapter Six*.

How Can They Be 'Experts' If They Often Mis-Diagnose?

Whilst the ICD is a separate manual to the US based DSM – the two often share similar criteria for making a diagnosis and if you are thinking the above diagnostic process seems incredibly imprecise – you are not on your own.

In the US, the *National Institute of Mental Health* (NIMH) completely withdrew support from the DSM-5 by stating that the newly introduced manual lacked 'validity' because it failed to use an 'objective laboratory measure' when compiling the diagnostic criteria for each 'disorder' – in other words it was too subjective and imprecise.

This is a huge blow to the credibility of the DSM and the current clinical diagnosis process in general (the ICD is based on similar criteria to the DSM). If you want to find out why this might signal the end of the DSM in its current form and a revolution in the diagnosis of autism, *'The End of the DSM?'* segment of *Autism: The Clinical Diagnosis Process (US)* found in the next section will provide more background to this debate.

Private Diagnosis Pathway

Those unhappy with the outcome of the NHS diagnosis may find themselves paying for a second opinion from a private clinician.

Pros & Cons Of Private Diagnosis

Pros

• A private diagnosis will not appear on any official medical records and thus can be kept truly 'private' if required.

• Some charity-funded autism services may accept a private diagnosis even if you have been unable to obtain an NHS diagnosis.

Cons

• This is an expensive option as full private medical fees will be charged.

• Many publically-funded autism services won't recognise a private diagnosis and will require an NHS diagnosis.

• There is no guarantee you will get an autism diagnosis.

• The risk of mis-diagnosis is still present.

Autism: The Clinical Diagnosis Process (US)

US clinicians refer to The American Psychiatric Association (APA) Diagnostic and Statistical Manual (DSM-5) which recognises autism as follows:

Autism Spectrum Disorder (ASD)

Persistent deficits in social communication and social interaction across multiple contexts.

Restricted, repetitive patterns of behavior, interests, or activities.

Changes Introduced In The DSM-5

The fifth edition of the DSM was introduced in 2013 and saw 'Asperger Syndrome' removed as a diagnosis. 'Asperger's' is now being phased out as an official diagnosis in the US clinical system as it has been collapsed into the broader term of 'Autism Spectrum Disorder'.

A person previously diagnosed with 'Asperger Syndrome' would now likely be diagnosed as having an 'Autism Spectrum Disorder' in an attempt to recognise that these traits form part of a wider 'autism spectrum' not a separate 'syndrome'.

The DSM-5 now asks diagnosing clinicians to 'grade' autistic traits by severity ranging from 'requires support' to 'requires very substantial support'. In theory this could be interpreted as a positive step towards recognising that autism is a wide spectrum with each person requiring different levels of support in adapting to a non-autistic environment.

In addition, in recognition that autism can be a sensory difference the DSM-5 has included different sensory processing as part of the diagnostic criteria as follows:

Hyper- or hyporeactivity to sensory input or unusual interests in sensory aspects of the environment (e.g. apparent indifference to pain/

temperature, adverse response to specific sounds or textures, excessive smelling or touching of objects, visual fascination with lights or movement).

Whilst the above could be considered a positive step, the DSM-5 may have hindered its goal of reducing autism 'sub-groups' by introducing a new diagnosis of 'Social Communication Disorder'.

A person diagnosed with this will not have the 'differences in sensory processing' or 'repetitive behaviors and/or restricted interests' unique to autism but will display many of the social communication differences of an autistic person. This person will not be diagnosed as autistic; thus reducing access to autism specific services.

As this new diagnosis has only recently been introduced, it is too early to assess the impact of this decision and how many autistic people are being mis-diagnosed with this new 'disorder'.

The End Of The DSM?

In 2013, two weeks before the DSM-5 was published, the *National Institute of Mental Health* (NIMH) distanced itself from the manual when its Director Thomas Insel authored an article which stated that the DSM-5 had a 'lack of validity' and 'Patients with mental disorders deserve better'.

The key issue? NIMH had tired of the DSM failing to use an 'objective laboratory measure' when compiling the diagnostic criteria for each 'disorder'.

In re-orienting its research away from DSM categories and advocating their own *'Research Domain Criteria (RDoC)'*, Insel states that NIMH is committed to new and better treatments that will arise from 'developing a more precise diagnostic system' – in other words the current diagnosis of mental disorders in the DSM-5 appears to be so imprecise that NIMH can longer endorse it.

This is a huge blow for the DSM with many in the industry predicting this signals 'the beginning of the end' of the manual as they know it.

Whilst the new model of 'biological psychiatry' being explored by NIMH remains untried and untested as it relies on a detailed understanding of the brain currently beyond the reach of the medical sector, the acknowledgement that the diagnosis of autism (and the other 'disorders' covered) is incredibly subjective and holds no 'validity' unless it is accompanied by a complete understanding of the brain *and* has been borne out by objective laboratory measures is a good start.

This verdict is hugely damaging to the credibility of the DSM (although it is still in use), yet in the long-term it may put an end to the frequent tendency for mis-diagnosis and the completely subjective approach to diagnosing autism; with a whole new view of it arising…

For those of you still interested in exploring a DSM-based clinical diagnosis, below is some more information on the diagnosis process.

Adult Autism Diagnosis Pathway

In 2014 the US Federal Government issued a directive that Medicaid plans must cover a full range of ASD services under the Early and Periodic Screening, Diagnostic and Treatment (EPSDT) provision in children up to age 21.

However, it is still difficult to get private insurers to cover autism-related services and adults over the age of 21 find it very difficult to obtain a diagnosis either with public or private insurance cover.

Those who do manage to obtain a Medicaid or private insurance diagnostic appointment will find the procedure similar to the UK system with some variances:

- The clinician may use diagnostic tools including DISCO (Diagnostic Interview for Social and Communication Disorders), the ADI (Autism Diagnostic Interview) or the ADOS (Autism Diagnostic Observation Schedule); or none of these.

• The US diagnosis process can often take place over two or three sessions; not just a single session as often happens in the UK.

• Since 2013 under the DSM-5 criteria individuals with ASD *must* show 'symptoms' from early childhood and so particular attention will be paid to this area during the diagnostic appointment.

Pros & Cons Of Formal Diagnosis

Pros

• A formal diagnosis makes it easier to access autism support groups and specialist support services (where available).

• A formal diagnosis provides eligibility to apply for disability benefits.

• A formal diagnosis makes it more difficult for people to challenge your autistic status.

• Some people find it comforting to have a formal diagnosis.

Cons

• If you are clinically diagnosed as autistic that means you are classed as having both a 'mental disorder' *and* a 'developmental disability'. This can be an issue if you ever come into contact with 'official bodies' or want to challenge the way you have been treated in a healthcare, education, legal or employment setting for example, as you may now find that your opinions are considered 'less valid' than they were before your diagnosis with some officials requesting an opinion from your specialist before granting you services that you have requested or making a decision on a complaint.

• Although a formal diagnosis should make it easier to access specialist support services in theory; in practice unless your insurance provides comprehensive coverage for follow-up services then contact with your diagnosing clinician often ends at the point of diagnosis. If a key reason for seeking a formal diagnosis is to receive support with understanding and managing your autistic traits and your insurance doesn't cover you beyond diagnosis, the lack of post-diagnosis follow-up support can be very distressing for a newly diagnosed autistic person. This is because you will often be notified about your diagnosis via a letter in the mail yet find yourself unable to discuss your diagnosis with the diagnosing clinician as you will most likely have been 'cut-off' from receiving any further support from them.

• It is not uncommon for adults with a formal diagnosis *and* insurance funding for follow-up support to find it difficult to locate a provider because their state has a limited number of certified autism specialists and their insurance will only fund services from a *certified* specialist.

• Most support services are targeted at autistic children with adult support groups extremely thin on the ground.

• The new DSM-5 criteria will result in some autistic people being mis-diagnosed as having a 'social communication disorder'.

• As evidence of autistic traits in childhood is a key criterion for diagnosis, some clinicians will refuse to diagnose an autistic person who does not bring a parent or sibling to the diagnostic appointment as they will be unable to assess your childhood traits.

Private Diagnosis Pathway

Adults who are unable to gain a diagnosis via their public or private medical insurance always have the option of paying for a private diagnostic assessment with the Pros and Cons of this option similar to the UK process outlined in the previous section of this guide.

Chapter 9

THE CHALLENGES OF AUTISM

If you have made it this far and are starting to accept that you may indeed be autistic, before you announce your new 'status' to the world there are a few things you may want to consider:

The Concept Of The 'Autistic Person'

The medical, legal and education sectors, the media and the general public generally do not understand the concept of the 'autistic person'. Most tend to view autism as a severe 'medical condition' which is separate to you as a person.

This is why you will tend to hear them say phrases such as 'she *has* autism' or he is 'a person *with* autism' as if autism is a 'condition' separate to the person.

To put this into context you wouldn't say 'John *has* homosexuality' or 'John is a person *with* homosexuality', you would say 'John *is* homosexual' – his 'homosexuality' is not a separate 'condition' to him as a person because it is hardwired into his genes; he is a *homosexual person.*

Although there is a growing movement of autistic people referring to themselves as an 'autistic person' and rejecting the view that they 'have' autism, some autistic people - particularly those who have been through the clinical diagnosis process will often use the phrase 'I am a person *with* autism' because this is what they have been conditioned to believe both by the medical sector and by those around them who don't know any different.

You may also find that some autistic adults seem to be unable to differentiate between their individual personality traits and their autistic traits or unaware that autistic traits vary from person to person. As a result they may make sweeping statements about autism which are not applicable to you.

Why Does This Matter?

Viewing autism as a 'condition separate from the person' implies it can be 'cured and removed from the person'.

This view has given rise to a huge 'autism industry' of researchers and organisations looking for a 'cure' for autism when they should be focusing their resources on practical support for autistic people to help them find work as well as helping those with sensory sensitivities understand what aspects of their environment are likely to trigger them.

The Hunt For The Cure: The Growing Threat To Autism

The reason practical support for newly diagnosed autistic adults is so thin on the ground both in the UK and the US is because many of the clinicians within the 'autism industry' are involved in the race to find the all-important 'autism gene'.

These clinicians devote a large part of their funding and time resource to finding the 'autism gene', or conversely finding the 'autism cure' so that they can have a place in the medical history books as *'the one who found the gene' OR 'the one who found the cure'.*

Providing practical programmes to help autistic adults improve their interview technique and modify their communication skills to better adapt to a non-autistic work environment is of little interest to most clinicians and the organisation's who fund them; that's why they very rarely offer them.

Autism Speaks Want To 'Cure' You

US organisation *Autism Speaks* is one of the best-funded autism charities in the world.

In '*The Autism Issue*' of *The New Idealist* magazine I authored an article entitled '*Why Autism Speaks Doesn't Speak For Autistic People*' (you can download *The Autism Issue* for free at www.amiautistic.com).

This article explored the organisation's stated view as being the:

*"world's leading autism science and advocacy organization, dedicated to funding research into the causes, **prevention**, treatments and a **cure** for autism" (emphasis added).*

You'll notice it doesn't actually refer to itself as a charity (although it is legally registered as such).

This might explain why its 2013 accounts show that *Autism Speaks* spends approx. 3.5 times as much money on '*science grants and awards*' ($15.3m) to meet its stated goal of finding a 'cure' for autism as it does on '*family service grants and awards*' ($4.6m). These amounts are then dwarfed by the $50.6m the organisation spends on 'advertising' (including donated media) to help propagate its message that autism needs to be '*prevented, treated or cured*'. This skewed spending results in the organisation generating over $120m dollars a year in donations yet spending less than 5% of that figure on offering practical support to autistic people.

This is typical of '*The Autism Industry*' – more money and resource goes into genetic research to find a 'cure' or towards the development of pre-pregnancy or prenatal tests to help prevent autistic babies being born than where it is needed most; practical support services for autistic children, adults and their families.

Google – *Don't Be Evil*

Even *Google* have now joined the 'race to the find the autism gene' by partnering with *Autism Speaks* on their *Ten Thousand Genome Program (AUT10K)* project which the charity hopes will help find a possible 'cure' for autism.

This is the same *Google* who gave themselves the official slogan of *'Don't be Evil'* and who must have employed hundreds of computer programmers with autistic traits in the development and improvement of their search algorithm.

In November 2014 CNBC published an article entitled *"Can Google find the cure for autism?"* which explained how this partnership sees *Google* providing the vast cloud-based database that researchers will use to upload the complete genomes of 10,000 autistic people and their families before sharing their genetic information to look for specific 'autism genes'.

Where did these genomes come from?

It transpires *Autism Speaks* has been collecting genomes from autistic people and their families for the last 15 years.

This then raises the question of whether or not the autistic children and adults whose genetic data has been 'scraped and uploaded' to *'Google's Cloud'* consented to being part of an international search for a 'cure' for autism?

Do they know their genes are now likely to be used for gene therapy 'treatments' designed to prevent other autistic people from being born?

I interviewed Stan Lapidus, CEO of *SynapDx Corp* for *The Autism Issue* as he runs a bio-science company developing a blood test for the early detection of autism in young children. During our interview he discussed how *Google Ventures* (the investment arm of *Google*) had invested in his company to help develop a blood test for autism.

In July 2013 *SynapDx* published a press release entitled:

'*SynapDx Corporation Secures $15.4M in Funding Led by Google Ventures*'

The release announced the appointment of *Google's* Andrew Conrad, PhD (Head of *Google X's* Life Sciences team), to the Board of Directors at *SynapDx*.

In the release *Google's* Conrad commented:

"*SynapDx stands to revolutionize the autism field while building the pediatric genomics company.* **Given my prior involvement on Autism Speaks' board***, I am well aware of the need for better diagnostics to help clinicians and families get children identified as quickly as possible*" *(Bold emphasis added)*.

This statement reveals that the current Head of *Google's* Life Sciences division is a former member of the *Autism Speaks* board.

The release also contained a quote from Krishna Yeshwant, MD, General Partner at *Google Ventures*:

"*SynapDx's use of advanced technologies and multiple analytes to generate the most informative blood test possible is a great example of the type of industry-altering innovation we look for at Google Ventures. Andy and I look forward to focusing on this important mission and accelerating the company's growth.*"

It seems that *Google* are now a full member of *'The Autism Industry'* and joining in *'the race to find the gene'* whilst viewing their investment in autism-related genetic research as a way of boosting their bottom line.

I asked Lapidus what made *Google* decide to invest in *SynapDx* and this was his response:

"So, in a sense, the smartass answer is ask Google, but I'll give you my version. We asked the question after they invested of "why did you invest?" It was a question I was afraid to ask right before they'd invested. The answer had three parts. It was a problem they have recognised as a large problem [...] mental health issues and autism in particular. They were fascinated, as we are, that multi-analyte markers – DNA, RNA and others, together – might break the path of a problem that's been unbreakable; that is to say, it's a math problem, and they're really good at math. We like to think we are too. So it's a big problem. It's one that captures Google's strengths, its own strengths, its own wisdom – you know, analysing large data sets – we do work with them on data analysis...

It's a problem that scales, which is a word of Google parlance that means if you're successful you can go from small to large rapidly, which is absolutely true.

And the third [reason] is that they were very intrigued by the people with whom we surrounded ourselves. In the company we have an outstanding team of accomplished individuals, and our [...] clinical science guys and advisors are all among the top scientists and clinicians in the field."

Why do *Google* seem to have such interest in funding blood tests for autism and supporting research to find the autism gene?

As Lapidus himself says; *maybe it's time someone should ask them.*

No 'Cure' Required Thank You

If you are autistic and you feel quite strongly that you don't need to be 'cured', the clinical and media fascination with a hunt for the autism 'cure' is one of the challenges of being autistic you will have to deal with whether you are self-diagnosed or formally diagnosed.

The Autism System – Why Does Autism Have Such Bad PR?

If you are aware that you have *positive* autistic traits and skills; *alongside the ones which cause you challenges* and are wondering why autism has such a negative image I have enclosed a brief summary of the workings of *'The Autism System'* (courtesy of that systemising trait I discussed earlier) to provide some background as to why the word *autism* generates such bad PR:

The Origins Of 'The Autism System'

> • The word 'Autism' (taken from the Greek word 'Autos' meaning 'Self') was created by a <u>medical clinician</u> to provide a name for a specific set of traits he saw in some of his patients.

> • The *Medical Sector* are the <u>creators</u> of the current *'Autism System'.*

> • As the creators of the system, they <u>set the rules of the system</u>.

> • The *defining rule* is that autism is classed as an <u>'mental illness/disorder/condition'</u> and is therefore nearly always viewed in *negative* terms both clinically and in the media and wider population.

> • A secondary rule is that as a 'disorder', autism needs to be <u>'treated', 'prevented' or 'cured'</u>.

> • The *defining rule* results in a <u>'top-down' system</u> with the clinicians who designed the system positioning themselves at the top with clinically diagnosed autistic people positioned <u>beneath them</u> 'under their care'.

• A side-effect of the 'top-down' system is that medical clinicians are then in a position to <u>speak 'on behalf of' autistic people</u> in the media because they are the 'experts'. In doing so they then propagate their negative view of autism.

• The *Autism System* has a variable which <u>gives more weight to 'status' over 'support'</u>; as a result finding an 'autism gene' or 'cure' for autism will attract more 'status' than providing 'support' in the form of practical support programmes for autistic people.

• The above variable skews resource towards status-driven genetic achievements as opposed to ground-level practical support programmes.

• The end result is that those who are diagnosed receive minimal post-diagnosis support as the *Autism System* prioritises *'autism science' over 'autism support'.*

• **The Autism System doesn't want to support Autism; it wants to cure it**

Beware 'The Desk-Based Autism Expert'

Some clinicians work on the 'frontline' and are committed to developing practical support programmes for autistic children and adults because they genuinely want to help those who struggle to adapt to a non-autistic environment.

Many are focused on genetic research.

If you read an article with a quote by an 'autism expert' and you want to know what their motivations are, one benefit of the clinical system is that it is possible to 'see' whether a clinician is primarily motivated by the grass-roots support of autistic people or by furthering their own 'science' career by looking up their current research interests online.

If you find the academic institution they are affiliated to, or locate their personal practice website their bio will list their current and previous research interests.

This enables you to assess whether they are primarily focused on furthering their status with 'genetic research' or whether they are motivated by helping autistic people with 'grass roots' practical support programmes.

Clinicians working to support autistic children and adults should have some current research interests that cover areas such as 'improving assistive communication between autistic children and their parents' or 'labour market integration for autistic adults' for example.

Where they have both listed – always look for their *current research interests*.

In addition it is useful to consider whether the 'expert' spends most of their time on the 'frontline' with autistic adults/children or whether their job primarily involves sitting at a desk analysing genetic data or doing desk-based research which *doesn't require any contact with autistic people* (which seems to be the case with most 'experts').

If the public and the media knew how little time the army of 'desk-based autism experts' actually spent in the same room as the autistic people they are meant to be 'experts in', questions might start to be asked about whether they are indeed 'experts' at all.

Autism Discrimination

If you decide to disclose your new autistic status to others you may find yourself subtly or overtly discriminated against.

Some ignorant people will talk to you or about you as if you are somehow less of a 'person' than they are. They may cease to take your view or opinion seriously and may view you or talk about you in derogatory terms.

A painful example of how the views of autistic people can be deemed 'less valid' than that of non-autistic people is when Adrian Palmer, a 21 year old British man with a diagnosis of Asperger's contacted police to say that he had been raped.

The police decided not to prosecute after the Crown Prosecution Service stated: *"He was not a credible witness due to his mental health issues".*

It has been reported that Adrian was receiving threatening phone messages from the alleged rapist and subsequently left his home town to stay in Wales. On his return - four months after the initial allegation of rape was made - Adrian was found dead.

He had been strangled and left in a street.

A local man was subsequently convicted of Adrian's manslaughter (no-one was convicted of rape), yet only served two years' in prison.

One of the reasons for the shamefully short sentence may be because Adrian had contacted and met up with his alleged rapist (who would later admit killing him) on his return. At the trial Adrian's mother said that her son's Asperger's meant that he didn't want there to be any animosity between him and his alleged rapist and this is why he got in touch with him on his return to the town.

An investigation by the Independent Police Complaints Commission found two officers guilty of misconduct due to their handling of the case and the report set out recommendations to help the police force deal with autistic and vulnerable people in the future.

Recently, there has been some deeply discriminatory and poorly-researched articles published in the mass-media linking the social differences found in autism to the 'anti-social' behaviour found in mass-murderers and serial killers. As a result, the next time a heavily armed psychopath decides to let loose on a school classroom or shopping mall you might need to prepare yourself for another slew of discriminatory articles stating that the killer was *'thought to have autism'* as he had *'difficulties making friends'* alongside a convenient *'What is Autism?'* graphic. No formal diagnosis seems to be required for this observation to be made and even if there was a diagnosis, those who read the previous chapter on the 'Clinical Diagnosis Process' might be wondering if the clinician mis-diagnosed psychopathy as autism due to the socially reclusive traits which can be found in both. In linking the anti-social traits inherent in psychopathy to autism without distinguishing between the two, most articles completely miss the point that many studies show that autistic people are more likely to be the *victims of a crime* rather than the perpetrators of one.

(All links to the news stories mentioned here can be found in the References & Further Reading section of this guide).

Autism Discrimination, The Media & The 'Seinfeld' Problem

Some of you may be aware that in late 2014, Jerry Seinfeld - one of the world's most successful comedian's - seemed to announce to *NBC News* that he was on the autism spectrum stating: *"I think, on a very drawn-out scale, I think I'm on the spectrum...Basic social engagement is really a struggle. I'm very literal, when people talk to me and they use expressions, sometimes I don't know what they're saying...But I don't see it as dysfunctional, I just think of it as an alternate mindset."* .

It seems fair to say that Seinfeld was not prepared for what came next...

Parent groups representing autistic children with learning difficulties berated him by stating that he *couldn't possibly be autistic* as he didn't have learning difficulties and that his presence as a 'successful performer' was hurting their cause and fight for their severely disabled children – they felt that his successes were undermining their challenges.

AM I AUTISTIC?

A particularly 'unpleasant' website which considers itself the place for news on the 'autism epidemic', published a post entitled *'Screw You, Jerry (Seinfeld "Autistic?")* stating that: *"He is arguably the world's most famous living comedian. And yet Jerry Seinfeld now claims he has autism."* Followed by the comment: *"Thanks, Jerry, for minimizing my son's disorder to the lowest possible level so that people don't take his special needs seriously."*

On the other side, some autistic advocates welcomed him to the spectrum only to then apply pressure in expecting him to 'represent' their views and political causes – *immediately.*

These advocates seemed to forget that the comedian is an *entertainer* – not an activist – and that he may well have just wanted to 'be' on the spectrum without getting involved in the 'politics' – as is his choice.

In any case, he would have needed some time to adjust to his newfound 'status' himself in the first instance before he would have been ready to represent the entire autistic population and our diverse range of political & social campaigns (if indeed anyone could ever be 'ready' for that!).

With all the 'instant pressure' following the announcement, is it any wonder a week later Seinfeld promptly u-turned and said he didn't now feel that he had a place on the spectrum?

Talking to *Access Hollywood*, Seinfeld retreated on his earlier comments stating: *"I don't have autism, I'm not on the spectrum...I just was watching a play about it and... I related to it on some level ... that's all I was saying."*

Whilst we have to accept that Jerry Seinfeld is not now on the spectrum, this saga really illustrates the difficulties that successful 'invisible autistics' have in making their status known.

AM I AUTISTIC?

The Misrepresentation Of Autism & Learning Difficulties

The organisations, clinical specialists and pharmaceutical companies who make up *The Autism Industry* seem to prefer that the *minority* of autistics (those with learning difficulties) are seen as the *majority* in the media, with discussion of 'professional autistics' being erased from the conversation entirely.

When they do highlight successful autistics it will generally be in the form of a child with severe learning difficulties making small improvements – which whilst important, still makes sure to associate autism with learning difficulties.

It should be made clear that what a lot of these groups term 'learning difficulties' is actually rooted in non-verbal behaviour. There are many autistic children (and adults) with 'learning disabilities' whose main 'crime' is that they don't speak. Many within this part of the spectrum respond well to 'assistive technology' (e.g. specially designed communication apps on tablets) and are happy to communicate in that way.

The American autistic teenager Ido Kedar is as good example of this. Ido is non-verbal and communicates via typing into an iPad which speaks his words out loud. Ido had to fight to attend his local high school and receive a regular education where he is now on the honors roll due to his academic merits.

In a great example of positive reporting from the mainstream media, when an NBC news crew filmed Ido, he communicated that he wanted people to know that: *"not speaking is not the same as not thinking"*. He has also commented that: *"It was terrible having experts talk to each other about me, and to hear them be wrong in their observations and interpretations, but to not be capable of telling them."*

(A link to Ido's blog and the news clip can be found in the References & Further Reading section at the back of this guide).

There are some very intelligent non-verbal autistics who have achieved college degrees, written books and run blogs – they are not in any way 'intellectually disabled'. It could be argued that this particular part of the spectrum is simply communicating in their own way and don't have any 'learning difficulties' at all – different is not disordered.

Those with learning difficulties in the area of severe toileting issues ect, really do seem to fall in the minority on the spectrum – although *The Autism Industry* makes sure to put them forward as *representing autism,* with some quarters responding incredibly aggressively when statistics or examples to the contrary are pointed out.

Disclosing Your Autistic Status

I disclosed my autistic status to a journalist from a major newspaper who I had previously come into contact with whilst researching *'The Autism Issue'*, after they referred to autism as a 'psychiatric disorder'. We ended up having quite some debate about the clinical definition of autism being classed as a 'psychiatric disorder'.

The reason the journalist's view mattered was because in addition to writing influential articles on autism for a major newspaper, they are also a researcher working on genetic research by developing *'techniques to identify biomarkers in autism'* (this title has been abbreviated to retain the confidentiality of the journalist).

As the journalist heavily subscribes to the <u>negative clinical view of autism</u> I was concerned that may influence the way they report autism in the future.

When you come across someone with an unrelentingly negative view of autism the only thing you can do is politely but firmly present your view and then exit the conversation; the only reason I entered into a debate with this person at all is because they are a journalist who writes articles which are read by millions of people who may be influenced by what they say *and* they are involved in genetic research into autism.

Had this have been a casual conversation at a social event I would have politely stated my view that autism is not a 'disorder' and every autistic person is different. If they then repeated their negative stance I would have simply ignored them or walked away as I have a policy of not spending any time trying to convince an 'autism negative' person any differently; I would rather just leave them to their ignorance and spend time with other people in the room who have developed a more rounded view of autism.

I take this approach because I have seen autistic contacts of mine become 'hypersensitive' to how other people view them and as a consequence get into terrible rows with people who air negative views and whilst I understand their frustration - it just isn't a healthy situation to be in.

Many people (particularly in the US; less so in the UK), refer to autism as a 'Disease'. This may have originated from autism being classed under *'The Centers for Disease Control and Prevention'* - the National Public Health Institute of the United States (the same people who held responsibility for containing the Ebola outbreak of 2014 when it reached US shores).

Stan Lapidus, CEO of Synapdx (the company researching the autism blood test which Google Ventures has invested in; as outlined in the previous section) has previously made scientific breakthroughs with PAP tests for cervical cancer and a DNA-based screening test for colorectal cancer.

Stan referred to autism as a 'disorder' throughout our interview (in line with the clinical view) and previously commented on autism research when speaking to a different magazine: *"Along the way the question from the diagnostics perspective has been 'What causes the disease'"*

Being labelled as having a 'disease' or 'disorder' is the sort of thing you will have to deal with if you disclose your status so don't do it until you are strong enough to handle negative views.

You will read comments from 'specialists' in the press or see them on the news talking about new 'treatments' or possible 'cures' for autism and many adult autistics do find this quite distressing/frustrating.

Unfortunately, having a full on row with 'Dave from accounts' in the staff room because he said something about hoping they find a cure for autism isn't going to help your cause, so it's best not to disclose your status until you are in a strong enough position to handle the discrimination which may follow.

Is Autism A Disability, A Disorder Or Neither?

The personal view of this author is that for the majority of the spectrum who are able to live independently; autism in itself is not a disability but can become one when the autistic person is forced to live and work in an environment which hasn't been adapted to accommodate autistic traits and preferences.

For the professional autistic with many autistic strengths, autism can temporarily become a disability when it gets in the way of your work or your social life.

Whether it's a minor impairment which results in an ability to only sit through one seminar at a whole day business conference due to the intense atmosphere and tightly packed seats running the risk of triggering a sensory overload (as is the case for this author), or if the pathway to workplace promotion becomes blocked due to the lack of preference for small talk with management, or if communication differences make it difficult for the autistic person to find a partner; if your autistic traits are preventing you from achieving things that you may otherwise have achieved if you *weren't autistic* – at that moment in time being autistic is definitely a *disability.*

Many professional autistics like the geeky programmers working in a computer company with other geeky programmers will not consider themselves disabled in any way because they have <u>structured their life</u>

<u>around their strengths</u> and have people around them who support them and their 'ways'; this further illustrates why *autism is a spectrum.*

Whilst autistic advocates are sometimes 'split' on the debate as to whether or not autism should be defined as a disability;<u> nearly all agree that autism is *not* a 'mental disorder'.</u>

Autistic people simply have different brain wiring and <u>different is not disordered.</u>

This author (along with other autistic advocates in the US and the UK) will continue to challenge this negative view of autism and campaign for autism to simply be referred to as 'autism'.

In the meantime, it is of some concern that the relentless negativity directed toward autistic people (particularly those who have been clinically diagnosed as having a 'disorder') can become a sort of 'self-fulfilling prophecy' in some ways; if society keeps telling someone they are 'disordered' they might start to think they are.

Hopefully those who read this guide will think differently.

<u>Social Isolation</u>

If your communication style makes it difficult to make friends, you have major sensory sensitivities which make it difficult to leave the house or you just find it too exhausting trying to not say the wrong thing at a social event, then you may find yourself withdrawing from society and retreating to the safety of your own home.

Adult autism support groups can help if there is one in your local area, however they are not typically geared towards the specialist requirements of the *professional autistic* and the difficulty accessing specialist support combined with the rejection of 'autistic traits' by others is a real issue for many adult autistics that is not easily solved.

What Next For The Professional Autistic?

The professional autistic represents a part of the autism spectrum particularly at risk of social isolation; everything seems fine on the outside – they may have a good job and a nice house but they may find themselves unable to connect to people beyond their work.

In this case a 'clinical diagnosis' of autism may not be particularly useful as even *if* diagnosed they will most likely fall between the cracks in the support services which are mainly geared towards autistic adults with *severe* and obvious communication impairments.

For the professional autistic the benefit of self-diagnosis is that it will help you to better understand why you are in this situation and provide a starting point for understanding your traits better:

> • Autistic people tend to bond with people over *shared interests* rather than small talk.

> • When you understand your traits better you should find it easier to avoid environments likely to trigger sensory overload and seek out environments which are relaxing for you and populated with people who share your *interests.*

> • By minimising time and energy trying to understand why you are not connecting to people who communicate differently to you or who you don't have much in common with, you will have more energy for exploring new areas and meeting people who operate on your wavelength who you *do* have things in common with.

The Importance Of Knowing Yourself

It's important to be aware of your traits and accept your autistic status because this is the only way you will begin to understand yourself. If you keep rejecting yourself you will be constantly in a state of 'flux' and at risk of sensory overload because you won't be managing the way you to respond to your environment; your environment will be managing you.

By ensuring you shape your world around *you* and your preferences instead of trying to fit yourself into the 'world' you are more likely to be fulfilled and find your 'home' as well as your place in society.

Although I didn't 'know' I was autistic until I turned 32, I've realised that I have subconsciously been working around my autistic traits ever since my experience of 'corporate politics' age 22. I've now had over 10 years' experience of shaping *my world* around my traits and preferences and I know what projects and environments I'm matched to and what I'm not matched to.

Life still throws curveballs (in my case having to wind down my career agency to avoid indirectly financing any more of *Google's* autism research would be a big one) and you can never 'control' all aspects of your environment – there are just too many variables.

It's best you view your life as 'work-in-progress' and take things one step at a time, and – *assuming you have some of the traits outlined earlier in this guide* – the first step is accepting you are autistic and this is why you are experiencing difficulties 'fitting in' with the rest of the world.

This first step is the biggest step and in my case it was a huge relief to know that there was a *specific reason* why my brain constantly overheated every time I went to crowded business exhibitions or when people who I don't know got too close to my 'personal space'.

Finding out I am autistic also explained why I always felt so fundamentally different and isolated from most people, yet often connected well to other people who shared similar interests to mine and liked discussing topics in-depth rather than in a superficial manner.

This realisation also helped me to understand why I 'see' the world the way I do with my systemising and visual thinking and why I am often able to spot details, patterns and trends that other people seem to miss.

Free Online Q & A

As there seems to be *zero* targeted support available for professional autistics (and little support for adult autistics in general), I will be adding a 'Q & A' section online in the future so those with questions about the self-diagnosis process as well as those seeking tips on how autistics can best handle interviews/job applications and working in a 'non-autistic' environment can post a question online (in confidence).

I can't promise I will have all the answers but it might be useful for those who want to talk to a fellow autistic about their experiences of living and working in a non-autistic world.

If you think you may be on the autism spectrum and have any questions about the self-diagnosis process, job-hunting or the workplace, please post your question online at www.amiautistic.com/ questions

Chapter 10

AUTISTIC GIFTS, TALENTS & SPECIAL ABILITIES

It seems appropriate for this guide to include a look at the unique strengths that autistic people can have. It is generally accepted that whilst an official diagnosis is not present, the following sample of inventors, physicists and technology world-changers all had *prominent* autistic traits:

- **Albert Einstein** – Physics Pioneer who developed the general theory of relativity and the concept of 'gravity'.

- **Nikola Tesla** – Electrical Engineering Pioneer who developed the alternating current (AC) electricity supply system still in use today.

- **Alan Turing** – Computer Science Pioneer, WW2 code-breaker and developer of the 'Turing machine' which laid the foundations for the developments in programming and computer science still in use today.

- **Steve Jobs** – Apple Co-founder and Technology Design & Marketing Pioneer who oversaw the design of the MAC, iPod, iPhone, iPad and the innovative Apple retail store concept.

The above represent a handful of the most influential pioneers with autistic traits and highlight the role that these traits have played in pushing the world forward; without autistic traits driving technical, scientific, engineering, artistic and math geniuses to work obsessively on finding solutions to societies biggest problems – or new ways of entertaining us – our world could still be in the dark ages.

Most people don't seem to be aware that there are many pioneers with prominent autistic traits *alive today* making huge contributions to the Arts, Science, Engineering and Technology sectors.

Most of these autistics are 'invisible' and the recent 'Seinfeld Announcement' and resulting firestorm that followed, illustrates the difficulties faced for those who do want to step forward.

The institutional misrepresentation of autism has led to it being seen as a 'taboo' in nearly every country across the world. As a result, many talented autistics will remain hidden with the rest of the 'invisible autistics', quietly making huge contributions to society without any recognition of their gifts and talents from the medical sector.

When you look at all the *positive* things autism has contributed to the world, it becomes more difficult to digest the way the medical sector talks about autism as no more than a set of impairments to be cured; without even an ounce of recognition that autism genes will most likely have brought them the computer they authored their report on as well as the phone in their pocket.

In the meantime, the race to 'identify and eradicate' the autism gene continues.

Let's Talk About The Positives

Of course most autistics are not geniuses but simply 'ordinary autistics' with an above-average attention to detail and a huge capacity for focus in our area of interest.

It has to be said that my work researching this guide has left me very concerned at how the strengths of autism are so often suppressed:

• The *medical sector* view autism as no more than an impairment to be cured, treated or prevented.

• Some *autistic advocates* try and suppress discussion about the *strengths* of autism as they fear that funding for disability benefits and/or support services may be reduced if the emphasis shifts to what autistic people *'can do'* instead of what we *'can't do'*. These advocates don't seem to realise that only promoting the *challenges* of autism helps to propagate the view in wider society that autism is something negative that needs to be 'cured' – the very thing they are advocating against.

• This topic even affected discussions I was having with a publisher who were very interested in acquiring the rights to this guide. Discussions broke down after they expressed 'concern' at this very section being included as discussing the strengths of autism was apparently *'slightly unnecessary and off-topic'*.

And Let's Not Forget About The Savants

And all of this before I've even mentioned the mysterious gifts of the Autistic Savant.

The truly amazing autistics who can memorise libraries of information and recall anything in an instant, musicians like Derek Paravicini who are blind yet can play entire pieces of music from memory after hearing them played just once and artists like Stephen Wiltshire *'The Human Camera'*, who draws huge panoramic scenes of the perfectly-recalled landscapes of huge cities after seeing them just once by helicopter.

There are those who will say *'not all savants are autistic'* – and they would be right. Some non-autistic people develop savant-like traits after a stroke or head injury, but this still doesn't explain why such a high proportion of savants are *autistic.*

AM I AUTISTIC?

For The 'Ordinary Autistics'

For those autistics and their friends and family who know we are not geniuses but simply ordinary autistics with positive traits which amount to more than a just a 'triad of impairments'; this section has been for you.

***

Chapter 11

WHAT NEXT?

The current crisis in psychiatry further strengthens the case for autism self-diagnosis.

If the supposed 'experts' can't even agree on a diagnosis of autism why should anyone trust their judgment?

In the eyes of the law, once clinically diagnosed an autistic person will remain legally 'under the care' of the medical sector - a medical sector who itself can't even agree on *what autism is* or how to address the challenges faced by those who are autistic.

Could the rise of the new phase of 'Biological Psychiatry' advocated by NIMH signal the end of autism being classed as a 'Mental Disorder' as it is currently and result in autism being classed as what it actually is; *a different brain type?*

Or, will this new wave of science along with pre-pregnancy tests like those being developed by *Pediatric Bioscience* bring *The Autism Industry* closer to its goal of finding a 'prevention' or 'cure' for autism?

Will the UK & US Government's lead the way in protecting future generations of autistic people by introducing new 'Anti-Eugenics' laws to prevent the development and marketing of prenatal and pre-pregnancy tests designed to eradicate the autism gene?

Or, will they stand by and do nothing.

Only time will tell.

Until Next Time

Stay tuned for future editions of this guide which will explore all new developments in the definition and diagnosis of autism.

I imagine in 20 years' time this guide will look quite different to how it does today.

I just hope it's for the better.

About The Author

Lydia Andal is a Journalist/Author, Publisher and Autism Advocate who works to promote a more balanced view of autism. Lydia has an older sister, three lovely nieces, two cats, a house in Manchester, UK and likes to take a break from 'politics' by finding great short stories as Founder & Editor of www.shortstorysunday.com.

Lydia is also an Ambassador for *Potential Plus UK,* a charity which raises awareness that gifted and talented children often find themselves socially and academically isolated. Without specialist mentoring and support many 'gifted' children fail to meet their potential when they could be making a great contribution to society; www.potentialplusuk.org

REFERENCES & FURTHER READING

This section is where you will find the links to the available facts/ evidence quoted throughout this guide as well as links to provide more 'background information' to some of the topics covered.

Autism Quick Facts:

http://www.cdc.gov/features/dsautismdata/

http://www.autism.org.uk/About-autism/Myths-facts-and-statistics/Statistics-how-many-people-have-autism-spectrum-disorders.aspx

Preface:

http://www.theguardian.com/science/blog/2014/may/01/prenatal-scrrening-test-autism-ethical-implications

http://www.utsandiego.com/news/2015/jan/15/autism-pediatric-biosciences-antibodies/

http://www.utsandiego.com/news/2013/jul/09/autism-maternal/

http://www.pediatricbioscience.com/mar_test/mar_test.html

http://www.pediatricbioscience.com/asd/asd.html

http://www.pediatricbioscience.com/pdf/discover_the_brain_fall2011.pdf

Judy Van de Water discusses her MAR research:

https://www.youtube.com/watch?v=ZnU-5fQ86g8

***The New Idealist* Back Issues are available for free download online at www.thenewidealist.com**

Issue Six – 'The Autism Issue'

Issue Five – 'The Doomsday Edition' *(Extreme Weather Special):*

Issue Four – 'The Issue We're All Talking About' *(With Game of Thrones and Last of The Mohicans actress Jodhi May as Guest Editor)*

Issue Three – 'Has Obama Been Corrupted By The Machine?'

Issue Two – 'IQ VS EQ – Is Emotional Intelligence What You Need To Succeed In The Digital Age?'

Issue One – 'Downwardly Mobile? Will The Next Generation Find It Harder To Reach The Next Level?'

Download the above issues free of charge via www.thenewidealist.com

Chapter 1 - The Plight of the Professional Autistic

https://www.autistica.org.uk/wp-content/uploads/2014/10/For-the-Hidden-Half-Million.pdf

http://www.imdb.com/title/tt2575988/ (Silicon Valley HBO TV Show)

http://www.autismresearchcentre.com/clinics

Chapter 2 - What is Autism?

http://claymarzo.com/

http://www.durbinrock.com/

http://www.news-sap.com/autism-and-aspergers-are-assets-not-disabilities-at-sap/

http://thedailyrecord.com/2012/09/09/autistic-lawyer-with-a-prize-winning-plan/

http://www.abcactionnews.com/news/local-news/ballet-student-diagnosed-with-aspergers-syndrome-dances-way-to-nutcracker-role#ixzz2lhvoUinU

Chapter 3 – Autism & The Autism Spectrum

http://neurodiversity.com/library_kanner_1943.pdf

http://www.lbhf.gov.uk/Images/Code%20of%20practice%201983%20rev%202008%20dh_087073%5B1%5D_tcm21-145032.pdf (P314 includes the definition of Autism as a 'Mental Disorder' in the Code of Practice for the UK Mental Health Act 1983).

http://www.autismrights.org.uk/drupal/node/23

http://www.awares.org/static_docs/about_autism.asp?docSection=3

http://www.autism.org.uk/About-autism/Autism-and-Asperger-syndrome-an-introduction/What-is-autism.aspx

http://www.nhs.uk/Livewell/Autism/Pages/Autismoverview.aspx

http://www.nhs.uk/conditions/autistic-spectrum-disorder/Pages/Introduction.aspx

http://www.nimh.nih.gov/health/topics/autism-spectrum-disorders-asd/index.shtml

Chapter 4 – A Guide to Autistic Traits

http://www.dailyrecord.co.uk/news/politics/revealed-secret-opinion-poll-convinced-4313922

Chapter 5 – A Guide to the Online Autism Diagnostic Tests

http://dsq-sds.org/article/view/1672/1599

Chapter 7 – Autism: the Self-Diagnosis Process

http://docs.autismresearchcentre.com/papers/2006_Wheelwright_etal_BrainResearch.pdf

http://www.theguardian.com/life/table/0,,937441,00.html

http://en.wikipedia.org/wiki/Hunter_vs._farmer_hypothesis

http://en.wikipedia.org/wiki/Attention_deficit_hyperactivity_disorder

http://www.independent.co.uk/arts-entertainment/music/features/boy-george-bad-karma-9185122.html

http://www.digitalspy.co.uk/music/s104/strictly-come-dancing/news/a605967/twitter-users-criticise-boy-georges-strictly-come-dancing-performance.html#~p2vOALJqEZWcoy

Chapter 8 – Autism, the Clinical Diagnosis Process

http://www.theguardian.com/lifeandstyle/2015/jan/05/are-women-with-autism-being-failed-by-nhs

http://www.dsm5.org/Documents/Social%20Communication%20Disorder%20Fact%20Sheet.pdf

http://www.dsm5.org/Documents/Autism%20Spectrum%20Disorder%20Fact%20Sheet.pdf

http://www.psychologytoday.com/blog/side-effects/201305/the-nimh-withdraws-support-dsm-5

http://www.nimh.nih.gov/about/director/2013/transforming-diagnosis.shtml

http://www.psychologytoday.com/blog/mood-swings/201305/nimh-requiem-dsm-and-its-critics

Chapter 9 – The Challenges of Autism

http://www.channel4.com/news/call-for-action-on-hate-crime-against-people-with-autism

http://www.ludlowadvertiser.co.uk/news/tenburywells/5038454.Tenbury_woman_speaks_out_over_events_leading_to_Adrian_Palmer_s_death/?ref=ar

http://www.dailymail.co.uk/sciencetech/article-2634865/Recipe-serial-killer-revealed-Childhood-abuse-autism-head-injuries-common-murderers-study-claims.html

http://www.autismspeaks.org/sites/default/files/documents/autism_speaks_2013_financial_statements.pdf

http://www.cnbc.com/id/102147046#.

http://magazine.thenewidealist.com/2015/07/09/issue-6-online-extra-autism-the-clinical-view-with-stan-lapidus-ceo-of-synapdx-corp/

http://www.fiercemedicaldevices.com/story/synapdx-attracts-6m-large-autism-dx-study/2012-12-11

http://www.theverge.com/2013/9/19/4748046/synapdx-blood-test-autism-google-ventures

http://www.synapdx.com/pdf/Synapdx%20Financing%20Announcement%207%2022%2013%20FINAL.pdf

http://blogs.wsj.com/digits/2014/07/25/meet-the-google-x-life-sciences-team/

http://www.nbcnews.com/health/mental-health/autism-advocates-hope-jerry-seinfelds-words-help-fight-stigma-n243636

http://www.ageofautism.com/2014/11/screw-you-jerry-seinfeld-autistic.html

http://www.accesshollywood.com/jerry-seinfeld-explains-autism-comments_video_2478937?utm_source=shortlink&utm_medium=Social&utm_campaign=video

http://idoinautismland.com/

http://www.nbclosangeles.com/news/local/Autistic-Teen-Writes-Book-on-an-iPad--204775591.html

Chapter 10 – Autistic Gifts, Talents & Special Abilities

http://www.bbc.co.uk/news/entertainment-arts-15086761

Thank you for reading

Am I Autistic? A Guide to Autism & Asperger's
Self-Diagnosis for Adults

2015 Print Edition

www.amiautistic.com

Printed in Great Britain
by Amazon